THE BIG BOOK OF
WOODWORK
PROJECTS

THE BIG BOOK OF
WOODWORK PROJECTS

More than 40 step-by-step designs for the home,
from beds to storage boxes, chairs to chests of drawers

ALAN & GILL BRIDGEWATER, PHILLIP GARDNER

NEW
HOLLAND

Published in 2007 by

New Holland Publishers (UK) Ltd

London • Cape Town • Sydney • Auckland

www.newhollandpublishers.com

Garfield House, 86–88 Edgware Road, London W2 2EA,
United Kingdom

80 McKenzie Street, Cape Town 8001, South Africa

Unit 1, 66 Gibbes Street, Chatswood, NSW 2067, Australia

218 Lake Road, Northcote, Auckland, New Zealand

ISBN 978 1 84537 315 3

Editor: Anne Konopelski

Production: Hazel Kirkman

Design: AG&G Books

Photography: Edward Allwright, Ian Parsons

Illustrations: Gill Bridgewater, Paul Griffin

Editorial Direction: Rosemary Wilkinson

1 3 5 7 9 10 8 6 4 2

Reproduction by Pica Digital Ltd, Singapore

Printed and bound by Times Offset, Malaysia

Contents

Tools and equipment

Woodworking is an incredibly rewarding activity, but only if you are using the right tools and equipment for the task. It's no good battling on with the wrong-size bandsaw, or trying to smooth wood with a plane that is dull-edged, and then deciding that woodworking is not for you. If you choose your tools with care, you will enjoy the experience of woodworking. Buy a basic tool kit to begin with and purchase additional tools when the need arises.

BASIC MACHINES

Traditionally, home woodworkers used hand tools – planes, saws, hand drills and so on – but there is now a shift to using small, basic machines to do some of the more tedious tasks. The following five machines are very useful: circular saw, planer-thicknesser, bandsaw, bench drill press and scroll saw.

Circular saw A circular saw is a machine for sawing stock to width and length. It is a table with a saw disc at the centre, a rip fence to the right-hand side and a sliding table to the left. To use it, you true up one edge of the wood, set the rip fence to the desired width, and then use your hands and a push-stick to move the wood through. It's a good machine if you want to reduce costs by converting rough-sawn boards to various plank and batten widths.

Planer-thicknesser A planer-thicknesser is a combination machine that is designed to plane all sides and edges of the wood square to each other, working through each in turn. Professional woodworkers generally use two machines – a surface planer and a thicknesser – but home woodworkers usually opt for a dual-purpose planer-thicknesser. There are many machines on the market, so spend time looking at the options.

1 **Circular saw:** *A circular saw is a useful machine, especially if you are going to do a lot of woodwork. It is mainly used for converting large boards into smaller sections, with the benefit of speed and accuracy.*

2 **Portable thicknesser:** *A thicknesser is used for reducing sections to the desired thickness (or width).*
3 **Surface planer:** *A surface planer establishes flat planed surfaces on a face and an adjacent edge.*

Bandsaw An electric bandsaw is a benchtop machine made up of a flexible, looped blade running over and being driven by two or more wheels. It is designed for cutting broad curves in thick-section wood. (Narrow blades suit tight curves in thin wood, while wide blades are better for broad curves in thick wood.) A small bandsaw fitted with a 10 mm blade is very useful.

Bench drill press The bench drill press – sometimes also called a pillar drill – is a machine dedicated to drilling holes. While you might think that a small, hand-held electric drill is sufficient for this purpose, a good-size bench drill press is better, because it enables you to bore accurately placed holes every time. To use it, you fit the bit in the chuck, clamp the workpiece to the drill table, set the depth gauge, and then pull the capstan wheel to bore the hole. A bench drill press teamed with a forstner bit is a combination that is difficult to beat.

Scroll saw The scroll saw is a fine-bladed electric saw designed for cutting intricate curves in wood. Before using it, the blade is tensioned, and then the workpiece is fed towards the blade. In order to saw out a shape in the middle of a piece of wood, one end of the blade is detached and passed through a drilled hole.

SPECIAL MACHINES

There are of course many other types of wood-working machine – everything from joint cutters, sanders and veneering presses through to spindle moulders, tenon cutters, large and small lathes, and plenty more besides. Novice woodworkers usually find that they soon develop an interest and expertise in a particular area, and then go on to buy appropriate small machines. For example, if you are interested in wood-turning, you might purchase a lathe, then a large, slow-wheel grinder to sharpen your turning tools. If you get hooked on joint-making, you might choose to buy a dedicated mortiser and a machine for cutting dovetails, and then a special machine to hone your chisels, and so on. Do not rush out straight away and start buying large lumps of machinery, because they might never get used. Also, don't be tempted to purchase small add-on attachments for your basic power tools (see page 8), because they can never perform as well as a dedicated machine. It is much better to borrow machines from your friends if they are necessary to follow these projects, and then to buy your own equipment when you fully appreciate your needs.

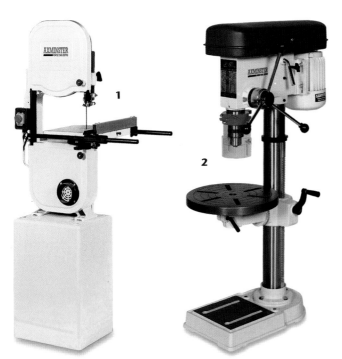

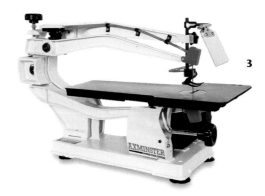

1 **Bandsaw:** *A bandsaw is ideal for reducing rough-sawn planks and cutting broad curves in thick wood.*
2 **Bench drill press:** *A bench drill press, used in conjunction with a forstner bit, enables you to make accurate, clean-sided holes.*
3 **Scroll saw:** *A scroll saw is the best machine for cutting tight curves and intricate fretwork designs.*

BASIC POWER TOOLS

Many novice woodworkers own an electric drill and various attachments such as a sanding disc, mini lathe, dovetail cutter and drill stand, all of which work in conjunction with the drill. The problem with these add-ons is that although they do work, to a greater or lesser extent, the results are usually so disappointing that the woodworker soon becomes disenchanted. My advice is to buy dedicated power tools, designed specifically to do a task, when you are confident that you can make good use of them. In the context of this book, the following six power tools are the ones to consider: cordless drill, jigsaw and sander (basic tools), router, mitre circular saw and biscuit jointer (special tools).

Cordless drill A cordless drill is a great tool, which is perfect for jobs where you don't want to be hampered by a trailing power cable. However, bear in mind that while a cordless drill does free the working area from power cables, the gearing of the drill requires that you work the holes in gentle stages, rather than single thrusts. At the end of the day, you have to remember to plug the rechargeable battery into the mains.

Jigsaw A jigsaw looks a little bit like a sander with a flat table on the underside, from which a blade protrudes. To use it, the saw table is set on the workpiece, with the blade not quite touching the wood to be cut, then the power is switched on and the tool is advanced. As the blade jiggles up and down, it swings from front to back so that it is clear of the wood on the down stroke. On most saws the table can be adjusted so that it tilts and allows you to cut at an angle of up to 45°. Some jigsaws are able to cut a thickness of up to 100 mm, so it is a very useful tool for most of the projects in this book.

Sander Modern sanders are really very sophisticated. You have a choice between wheel sanders, belt sanders, sanders with file-like fingers, random orbital sanders that fit in the palm of your hand, large high-powered sanders that are used for finishing wide areas, and so on. Consider buying two machines: a large, flat sander to work broad surfaces, and a little triangular palm-size sander to round over edges and get into tight corners.

SPECIAL POWER TOOLS

Router A router is designed to do all the tasks that were once achieved by using a whole range of planes. Not so long ago, grooves, moulding, rebates and tongues were cut with chisels and different-sized planes (with various universal and multi-planes coping with a number of tasks). Nowadays, a router does all these things. There are two schools of thought about routers. One says that they are wonderful; the other says that they are noisy, dusty, potentially very dangerous, altogether unpleasant, and the cutters are very expensive. Using a router may not be as much fun as using a plane, and the results may not be any better, but there is no denying that they are very much faster.

To perform the tasks, a router is fitted with cutters in various shapes and sizes, which are the reverse of the shape that you want to cut. So, for example, a tongue-shaped cutter will make a groove-shaped cut. A router can be used as a hand-held tool and run forward to make the cut, or it can be turned over and fitted in a router table, in which case the workpiece is moved so that it comes into contact with the cutter.

Mitre circular saw Strictly speaking, a power tool is defined as a smallish, hand-held tool such as a router, drill or sander, but some of the benchtop machines are now so small and portable that the distinction between them is becoming blurred. The mitre circular saw looks a bit like a cross between an angle grinder and a guillotine. It is primarily designed to crosscut, but you can also cut mitres and angles through to 45°. The length of timber is set on the table, the power is switched on and the blade is lowered or pulled across the wood.

Biscuit jointer The biscuit jointer, or biscuiter, is a versatile, easy-to-use tool. You simply make marks on the two pieces of wood that you want to join (edge to edge or at right angles), then set the jointer on the mark, press the button and push forward. This causes a saw wheel to make a groove. Next, you align grooves in both pieces of wood, fill them with glue, slide in a little biscuit-shaped piece of compressed wood, and clamp the wood together. This forms a reinforced joint.

Useful power tools: *1 Jigsaw for cutting curves, 2 Router for cutting grooves, joints and edge profiles (cutters: 3 Radius cutter for routing an edge profile, 4 Straight cutter for trimming edges, 5 Straight cutter for routing grooves and housings, 6 Chamfer cutter for routing a 45° bevel), 7 Palm sander for smoothing flat or shaped surfaces (with 8 Sanding sheet), 9 Rechargeable drill and screwdriver.*

WORKING SAFELY

Woodworking is potentially dangerous so always follow this safety checklist:
- Do not use machinery if you are too tired to concentrate or taking medication that makes you drowsy.
- Study the machine manuals.
- Keep electric cables and plugs on power tools in good condition.
- Let someone in the house know when you are using any machines.
- Make sure you are adequately protected with a dust mask, goggles and ear defenders (see page 11).
- If you have long hair, tie it back.
- Supervise children.
- Keep a first-aid kit nearby.
  - Be near a telephone in case of accidents.
  - Keep the workshop locked.

HAND TOOLS

Weekend carpenters need a good range of hand tools, including marking-out tools, saws, planes, chisels, hammers, mallets, knives and clamps.

Marking-out tools Woodwork starts with measurements and guidelines. You will need a tape measure, pencils and rule, a square, set square and bevel gauge for establishing angles, a pair of dividers for stepping off measurements, a pair of compasses for drawing circles, and a mortise gauge for setting out joints.

Saws The most useful saws to purchase are a tenon saw for sawing small sections of wood to length and for cutting large details, a gents saw for small joints, and a mitre frame saw for cutting angles. Always choose best-quality saws that can be re-sharpened.

Planes You need three planes: a good smoothing plane for levelling board widths, planing edges and for skimming the ripples that can occur on machine-planed wood; a block plane for cleaning up end grain and for planing through tenons flush with a surface; and a spokeshave for planing curves.

Chisels A set of good-quality chisels is essential. While there are all manner of chisels on the market, I recommend that you get yourself a set of bevel-edge chisels – the best that you can afford. It is also useful to have a sharpening stone.

Frequently used hand tools and drill bits:

1 Mallet, 2 Mitre frame saw, 3 Swift-release clamp, 4 Sash clamp, 5 Metal rule or straightedge, 6 Smoothing plane, 7 Pin hammer, 8 Bevel gauge, 9 Mortise gauge, 10 Square, 11 File, 12 Turning tool, 13 Spokeshave, 14 Block plane, 15 Tape measure, 16 Dividers, 17 Pair of compasses, 18 Pencil, 19 Large penknife, 20 Small penknife, 21 Forstner drill bit, 22 Cross-point screwdriver, 23 Twist bit, 24 Plug cutter, 25 Pilot-countersink bit, 26 Allen key wrench, 27 Long-nosed pliers, 28 Adjustable wrench, 29 Electric soldering iron, 30 Bevel-edge chisel, 31 Gents saw, 32 Tenon saw, 33 Small hacksaw.

Hammers and mallets Three different hammers are must-haves: a large claw hammer for hefty work and for pulling out nails, and a couple of different-sized pin hammers for all the small nailing tasks. A mallet is suitable for the times when you need to strike the wood or a tool and be certain that it will not damage it or leave a mark. A carpenter's square-headed mallet is ideal for tapping chisels; a heavy, round-headed mallet provides more weight, or is good when using carving gouges.

Knives Knives are extremely useful tools. A good selection might include a small penknife for whittling, an old chip-carving knife for marking out and for tidying up tasks, and a large, bevel-bladed knife for cutting dowels. Old knives, which can often be found in old junk shops, tend to keep their edges longer.

Clamps You can never have too many clamps. A selection of several long-beam sash clamps, a holdfast clamp on the workbench alongside the vice, one or two swift-release clamps, and a whole host of G-clamps all come in handy. Only buy the best, always get them in pairs, and don't be tempted to purchase them secondhand, or to buy cheap imports.

Metalworking tools As well as the woodworking tools, you will also need a small hacksaw for trimming nails and cutting threaded metal rod to length, a file for smoothing the sawn edges of these, and pliers for any number of tasks. (You can also use an electric soldering iron for pyrography: it is not really designed for the task, but it is safe and it does the job efficiently.)

OTHER TOOLS

Drill bits You need twist bits for drilling general holes, and large-size forstner bits to make special holes that form part of the design. If you can afford it, get yourself a whole range of forstner bits. They are expensive, but last well and cut a perfect hole every time. You will also need a pilot-countersink bit for drilling screwholes for countersunk screws, and a counter-bore bit and matching plug cutter for making a screw joint that incorporates a recess for a wooden plug.

Woodturning tools If you want to try your hand at woodturning, you will first need a lathe, plus a selection of woodturning tools including gouges for rouging out, a skew chisel for cutting grooves and for smoothing up, a parting tool for parting off, and a couple of scrapers for general smoothing and tidying up. Start by making do with the tools supplied with the lathe, and then get yourself a better range when you have more experience and can decide what you really need.

SAFETY EQUIPMENT

When working with machines that make a lot of noise and produce fine dust, you need, at the very least, to get yourself a basic dust mask, a pair of ear defenders and a pair of safety goggles. A full-face respirator is useful when you are working with the lathe. It allows you to wear glasses and also filters the air without pressing directly against your mouth. There is one further health consideration: sometimes exotic species of wood cause allergic reactions. Avoid this possibility by mostly limiting yourself to working with pine (American or European pine).

Safety equipment: *1 Full-face respirator with built-in visor, dust filter and air blower, 2 Ear defenders, 3 Dust mask for low levels of wood dust, 4 Goggles.*

Materials

It is best to purchase wood from a specialist supplier that only sells wood and related products and tools. Purchase your wood ready prepared, and as near as possible to the finished size. Inspect the wood on offer closely and reject pieces that are split, of poor colour, twisted, full of knots or in any way faulted. Go armed with a cutting list and a tape measure, and be clear in your own mind as to your needs. The ideal supplier is staffed by knowledgeable people, who are prepared to cut the wood to size without splintering the cut edges, and can ensure that all the edges are square to each other. Always ask for the offcuts.

WOOD TYPES

Swedish pine A straight-grained, creamy coloured softwood. It is easy to work, with an attractive grain texture and a minimum of knots – a perfect choice for many of the projects in this book.

Swedish laminated pine If you cannot get a board wide enough, use Swedish laminated pine. The pine is sawn into strips and glued to a prepared board width. It's a good product for component parts such as the sides of chests. Do not use laminated pine for outdoor furniture.

Ash A long-grained, tough, grey to red-brown hardwood traditionally used when there is a need for strength. A good choice for many of the projects.

Maple A creamy-coloured hardwood – perfect for modern furniture, such as the Kitchen trolley (see page 116). It cuts to a beautiful crisp finish.

American oak Also known as American red oak, this hardwood is pink-brown in colour, with a beautiful straight grain. It is very tough but easy to work.

American cherry A creamy pink-to-brown, fine-textured, straight-grained hardwood. It is expensive, but a good choice if you require a hard, shiny finish. Specify American cherry, because it comes in much wider boards than the European species.

American mahogany A red-brown, straight-grained, uniform-textured hardwood. Mahogany is an endangered species, so you may wish to limit yourself to using offcuts salvaged from old doors. It's a good choice for very small details.

READY PREPARED WOOD

Ready prepared wood is planed and squared on all faces to a set width. You can also order it sized, and it will be sawn to a set length. Softwood is often sold as PAR (planed or prepared all round). Be careful when you buy this, as the the size quoted is always of the sawn section. When the wood has been planed on all four faces to achive the PAR state, the section has been reduced by about 5 mm in both directions, so the 50 x 50 mm PAR is, in fact, about 45 x 45 mm. If you enjoy the prospect of sawing and planing, order your wood seasoned and sawn. When it comes to using tongue-and-groove boards, as in the French cupboard (see page 122), go for best-quality prepared double-sided pine boards.

PLYWOOD

Many of the projects in this book use top-quality birch plywood, which is a sheet material made up from veneer layers. It is easy to work – it saws and planes to a clean edge, and the light-coloured grain is attractive.

SAMPLES OF WOOD TYPES AND FINISHES

Wood types (and finishes): 1 Swedish pine (teak oiled), 2 Ash (teak oiled), 3 Maple (teak oiled), 4 American oak (Danish oiled), 5 American cherry (Danish oiled), 6 American mahogany (Danish oiled), 7 American oak (wire-brushed and oiled), 8 Swedish pine (colourwashed), 9 Swedish pine (acrylic paint).

FIXINGS

There are thousands of products on the market, but for simplicity's sake you may want to limit yourself to using steel and brass screws, nails and pins, plated steel threaded rod cut to length and used with washers and nuts, hex-head and toggle fasteners, wooden dowels, and plastic screw blocks. The brass hex-heads used with the toggles and threaded rod may be unfamiliar to you. If you look at the Adjustable porch chair on page 128, you will see how these beautiful fixings allow boards to be joined at right angles to each other, without the need to cut traditional joints, and with the added benefit that the structure can be disassembled for easy transport. Note that most modern fixings for making joints are designed to be hidden from view.

FITTINGS

The projects primarily use four fittings: two different-shaped hinges (surface-mounted and recessed), brass cuphooks, and swivel wheels. There is not much to say about these items, other than they are best purchased when the project has been made, so you can order a specific size and shape to fit the finished sizes. When you are buying hinges, obtain screws to fit at the same time. When it comes to knobs and handles, ones that have been whittled from scraps of wood – as used on the Bathroom cabinet (see page 86) and the French cupboard (see page 122) – are hard to beat. Select a promising piece of wood, either a piece of straight-grained pine or a piece of lime, then simply whittle away with a penknife until you have a shape you like.

Useful fixings and fittings: *1 Plastic joining blocks, 2 Brass cuphook, 3 Swivel wheel, 4 Wooden fluted dowel, 5 Brass hex-head nut, 6 Toggle fastener, 7 Nut, 8 Washer, 9 Threaded rod (available in 1 m lengths), 10 Oval-headed nail, 11 Galvanized flat-headed nail, 12 Black steel pin, 13 Brass round-headed pin, 14 Slotted round-headed screw, 15 Slot-headed countersunk screw, 16 Cross-headed countersunk screw, 17 Cross-headed, round-topped screw, 18 Surface-mounted hinge, 19 Recessed hinge with countersunk screwholes.*

GLUE

There are hundreds of types of glue on the market, but there is no technical reason why, for the projects in this book, you shouldn't use white PVA glue. Squeeze it straight from the plastic bottle and smear it over both mating surfaces, and then clamp up and leave to cure.

FINISHING

Fortunately, thick, brown, high-shine varnishes are no longer in fashion. Instead you can use traditional finishes such as teak oil and Danish oil, or colourwashes in conjunction with oil and beeswax. The trouble with varnish is that you have to be careful there aren't any dribbles, and make sure that dust doesn't settle during the drying process. With oil, you don't have to worry about these things. Teak oil and Danish oil, either wiped on with a cloth or applied with a brush, work well. Catalyst (two-part) lacquers are excellent spray finishes but unsuitable for the home workshop as special ventilation is required. Colourwash is made from acrylic paint thinned down with water. If you want to achieve a sheen finish, simply wait for the oil or paint to dry, rub down with graded sandpapers, and then burnish with pure beeswax polish.

Glue and finishing materials: *1 PVA glue, 2 Teak oil, 3 Acrylic colourwash, 4 Danish oil, 5 Buffing polishing cloth, 6 Lint-free cotton cloth, 7 Pure beeswax polish, 8 Sanding block, 9 Garnet paper, 10 Silicon-carbide paper, 11 Aluminum oxide paper, 12 Wire brush.*

Basic techniques

Woodwork is a bit like a journey. It is wonderful to set out, and just as exciting to reach your destination, but a good part of the enjoyment is in all the adventures between start and finish. It is a great feeling when you present family or friends with something that you have made with your own two hands, but many of the procedures and techniques along the way are just as pleasurable. It is very satisfying when you test the keenness of a razor-sharp edge, smell the wood and feel its texture, and then go on to make a crisp, clean cut. The following section will show you how to use your tools to achieve the various forms, joints and textures. If you are ever unsure about any procedures involving tools, or uncertain whether a type of wood is suitable, it is always a good idea to have a trial run on offcuts of wood. Try and keep the workshop shipshape – some woodworkers start a fresh project by cleaning and sharpening hand tools, tidying up the workshop and cleaning woodworking machines.

PREPARING PIECES OF WOOD

When you have decided what you want to make, take your carefully selected pieces of planed wood and sort them into groups. Mark each piece so that you know how it fits into the scheme of things, noting the top, bottom, best faces and edges. Use a pencil and rule to measure the lengths. Take a set square and run the marked points around the wood, so that you know which parts need to be cut away. Use a pair of compasses to set out curves and dividers to transfer measurements from drawings to the wood.

If you need to reduce the width of a board or set out a joint, adjust the marking gauge to the appropriate measurement and run the gauge along the wood to make a mark. Use the bevel gauge to set out lines that are going to run at an angle to an edge.

If you have pairs of components, mark them out at the same time so that they are identical (and remember to make them a mirror image of each other). When you are setting out a detailed joint, it helps if you score the lines with a knife. When you have set out all the lines that go to make up the design, it is often a good idea to shade in the waste side of the cutting line, so that you know precisely where to run the saw cut.

CUTTING CURVED SHAPES

To cut a curve, you have a choice of using a jigsaw, a scroll saw, a bandsaw or one of the hand saws. A jigsaw is best for cutting rough curves in thick wood, when the line of cut is well away from the edge of the workpiece (see Fig 1). Set the table part of the saw on the mark, switch on the power and advance to make the cut. Jigsaws have a tilting base, which changes the angle of the saw cut, and numerous types of blade are available to suit the type and thickness of a material.

FIG 1

Use a scroll saw for cutting fine curves in wood less than 50 mm thick (see Fig 2). Fit a new blade and adjust the tension until the blade "pings" when plucked. Set the workpiece on the saw table, switch on the power, and run the workpiece into the blade. If you feel the wood running off course, or you see the blade bending, ease back and readjust the direction of approach. If you need to cut out a window shape, then you can do one of two things. Either run the cut in from an edge or, to avoid cutting the wood surrounding the window, drill a hole through the waste, and then unhitch the saw blade, pass it through the hole and re-tension as already described.

out several times to remove the waste and to minimize overheating. If you are faced with drilling lots of holes in lots of identical component parts, as in the Sauna bench project (see page 96), it's a good idea to build a jig from offcuts (a "fence" and a "stop" screwed to a base board, which is clamped to the drill table).

An electric drill used with a twist bit is a good option when you want to drill screwholes and perhaps pilot holes for nails. If you have a choice, use a cordless drill, so that you don't have to worry about the cable snaking about the workshop. To drill, simply switch on the power, set the point of the bit on the mark, make sightings to ensure that the bit is square to the face of the item being drilled, and then run the hole through. When you have to put in a lot of screws (see Fig 4), a screwdriver drill attachment is very useful.

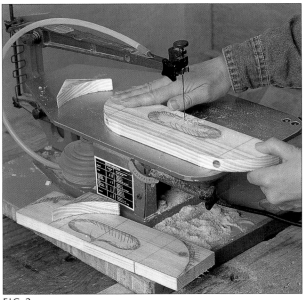

FIG 2

FIG 3

DRILLING HOLES

Use the bench drill press in conjunction with a forstner bit for drilling large holes that need to be precisely placed and worked (see Fig 3). Establish the centre of the hole, fit the appropriate size bit, set the depth stop and clamp the workpiece securely to the drill table. Clamping the workpiece takes a little extra time, but is worth doing because you can locate the hole more accurately, the finish of the hole will be better, and the procedure is safer. Lower the bit to ensure that the point is directly on centre, then switch on the power and run the hole through. If the hole is deep, lift the bit

FIG 4

HAND PLANING

Hand planing is a very satisfying procedure, as long as the plane is sharp and you take your time. A smoothing plane is ideal for working in the direction of the grain (see Fig 5) along edges and faces. Make sure that the workpiece is secure, turn the brass advancing wheel to set the blade, perform a trial cut to judge whether or not the blade is at the correct depth, and then make the cut. When you are working the edge grain, hold the plane at a slightly skewed angle, with the fingers of your left hand under the sole of the plane to ensure that the plane is square to the face of the wood.

FIG 5

The block plane is perfect for trimming arris (sharp edge) details (see Fig 6) and for tidying up end grain. Adjust the blade so that it makes the lightest of skimming cuts, have a trial on an offcut, and then make the stroke. When you are working end grain, be careful not to run off course and split the grain (see Fig 7).

FIG 6

FIG 7

HAND CUTTING A MORTISE

Having used a pencil, rule, set square and perhaps the point of a knife to set out the mortise, move to the bench drill press and use the appropriate size bit to bore out most of the waste (see Fig 8). Be careful not to drill too near the edge of the mortise. Shake the waste from the hole, secure the workpiece in the vice so that the face to be worked is uppermost, and then take a suitable bevel-edge chisel and pare back the hole to the edge of the mortise (see Fig 9). Hold the chisel upright so that you don't undercut the surface or damage the edges. When you are half-way through, turn the wood over and work from the other side.

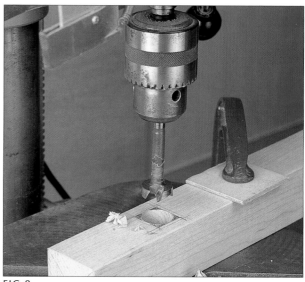

FIG 8

FIG 9

ROUTING A MORTISE

Depending on the size and position of the mortise, you can use a router to make the cut. Either use the router as a hand-held tool and plunge down to clear the waste or, for an open-ended mortise (see Fig 10), attach the router to its table and run a groove from one end of the workpiece. In this instance, the accuracy of the cuts relates to the setting of the fence and the height of the bit. Always test your settings by routing into an offcut (not a final component). It is best to cut the depth in stages, making several passes that do not overstrain the router. Make sure that you clear the waste after each pass to avoid overheating the bit.

HAND CUTTING A TENON

Begin by marking the shoulder-line (the length of the tenon) with a square and knife, and then mark the depth and width of the tenon with a marking gauge. Remove the waste with a tenon saw: first run a cut down the grain to the waste side of the gauged lines (stop the cut at the shoulder-line) on all four sides of the tenon. Cut across the grain to the waste side of the shoulder-line on all four sides, removing all the waste. Use a chisel to clean up the tenon and trim it to its proper size where necessary.

ROUTING A TENON

If you have a lot of tenons to make (or if you just like using machines), a router set in a table is the ideal tool for the job, as long as your pieces of wood are of a size that can be supported by the table (bigger pieces of wood are best clamped to the bench and routed by hand). All you do is set the fence to the length of the tenon, adjust the router bit to the appropriate height, then hold the workpiece hard against the push-fence and clear the waste with a series of passes (see Fig 11). When the end of the tenon reaches the fence, turn the workpiece over and re-run the procedure on the other side. If you stop just before the router bit reaches the shoulder-line, use a chisel to tidy up.

FIG 10

FIG 11

ROUTING A GROOVE
WITH THE GRAIN

To cut a groove that is 6 mm wide, 4 mm deep and lies 10 mm in from the edge of a board, follow these steps. Attach the router to its table and fit a 6 mm groove cutter. Set the fence to 10 mm. Adjust the cutter so that it stands 2 mm higher than the router table. Switch on the power and push the wood along the fence to cut a groove to a depth of 2 mm (see Fig 12). Switch off the power, and then set the cutter 2 mm higher and re-run the pass to cut the groove to 4 mm.

ROUTING A REBATE ON
THE END OF A BOARD

To cut a rebate that is 10 mm wide and 4 mm deep, follow this procedure. You need a straight cutter that is smaller than the width of the rebate – for example 5 mm. Put the router in the router table and fit the cutter. Set the fence 5 mm back from the rear edge of the cutter, and adjust the cutter height to 2 mm. Switch on the power. Hold the workpiece against the push-fence and make a cut that laps into the end of the board by about 5 mm. Re-run the cut – keeping the end of the board against the fence – in order to cut the full 10 mm width of the rebate. Switch off the power, adjust the cutter so that it stands 4 mm high, and repeat the sequence to complete the cut (see Fig 13).

ROUTING A HOUSING
GROOVE FREEHAND

Clamp the workpiece to the bench. Fit a router cutter that is either the same size or smaller than the width of the groove, and set the depth stop. Clamp a guide strip of wood across the workpiece to run parallel to the groove, so that the cutter will run up the waste side of the drawn line. Set the router down with the base pressed against the guide, switch on the power and wait until the cutter is up to speed, then make the cut. If the cutter is smaller than the groove, shift the guide strip closer and re-run the procedure until the groove is the correct width and depth (see Fig 14).

FIG 12

FIG 13

FIG 14

ROUTING EDGE PROFILES

Cutting an edge profile is one of the easiest routing procedures. Attach the router to its table and fit your chosen cutter – radius (see Fig 16), cove (see Fig 15), Roman or other type. Use one with a pilot or bearing roller-tip. Move the fence so that it is well out of the way. Switch on the power and wait until the router is up to full speed. Now press the workpiece down on the table and run it repeatedly against the cutter. Work with an easy, firm motion so that the cutter enters on the left and exits on the right. Continue until the workpiece rubs up against the pilot or roller-tip, at which point the cutter will cease to cut. If the profiled edge looks burnt, the router cutter might be blunt, or you may be moving too slowly across the wood.

FIG 15

FIG 16

ROUTING WITH A TEMPLATE

Use a template when you want to produce a number of identically shaped components with a smooth routed finish on all the edges. The components first need to be sawn roughly to the shape required, leaving no more than 4–5 mm of waste wood to be removed by the router. Fit a guide bush to the base of the router. Cut a template from sheet plywood, allowing for the collar, and pin it directly to the face of the wood that you want to cut. Switch on the power and wait for the cutter to get up to full speed, then follow the edge of the template to make the cut.

A similar, but more immediate technique for duplicating a component involves the router, a straight cutter with a bearing attached (the bearing can be at the top or bottom of the cutter) and the original finished component, which is used as the template. The procedure is the same as that described above.

CUTTING MITRES
WITH A FRAME SAW

The frame saw offers an easy way of achieving angled saw cuts. Adjust the saw blade within the frame to your chosen angle – 90°, 45°, 36°, 22.5° or 15° – and lock it in place. Set the depth stop to the chosen depth. Position the workpiece on the saw table, hard up against the fence, and then gently run the saw backwards and forwards to make the cut (see Fig 17).

FIG 17

NAILING AND PINNING

Look at the workpiece to decide whereabouts the nail or pin is to be sited. If it is near an edge or end, where there is a chance that the wood will split, or you want to ensure that the nail goes in straight, run a pilot hole through with an electric drill, using a bit that is slightly smaller than the diameter of the nail. Set the point of the nail in the hole and use an appropriate size hammer to drive it home. Give it a series of well-placed taps (see Fig 18), all the while watching to make sure that the point of the nail doesn't break through the other side. If it does run off course, use a pair of pliers or a claw hammer to draw it out. If you are using very small pins, which are fiddly to hold and hammer in, use a pair of long-nose pliers to grip the pin as you nail.

FIG 18

SCREWING

You have a choice of using mild steel, stainless-steel, brass or aluminium screws (either cross-headed or slot-headed) with various countersunk or domed heads. Dome-headed screws stand proud of the wood; countersunk screws are set flush with the surface, or held in a brass cup, or hidden by a plug of wood. Screws are driven in with a cross-point or flat screwdriver, either by hand or using an electric drill fitted with a screwdriver bit (see Fig 19). If you use a screwdriver bit in an electric drill, set the slipping clutch mechanism so that the screw is driven in to the correct depth. If the wood is

soft, you can spike a pilot hole with an awl (see Fig 20); if it is hard you can bore a pilot hole with a small drill bit. If you want to cover the screws with a wood plug, you will need a counter-bore bit to drill the pilot hole and the hole for the plug, and a matching plug cutter to cut the plug. It is best to practise the entire drilling and screwing operation on a piece of the scrap. Do not use steel screws for oak, because they react with the wood and moisture to leave a stain. Use plated steel, brass or stainless-steel screws instead.

FIG 19

FIG 20

WOODTURNING

If you want to make true round-section items such as chair legs, bowls and platters, the only way to do it is to turn them on a lathe. Buy the highest powered, heaviest lathe that you can afford – one with an expanding chuck and a selection of face plates. Spindles and cylinders are pivoted and turned between the head centre and the tailstock centre (see Fig 21), while bowls and dishes are generally turned on a flat face plate. The best lathes are fitted with a device that allows you to turn large face-plate items on the out-board end of the drive spindle (see Fig 22). You will need various turning tools: a gouge, parting tool, skew chisel and a round-nosed scraper. Lathes can be very dangerous, so always follow the safety instructions.

FIG 21

FIG 22

WHITTLING

All you need for whittling items such as door knobs and catches is a good, sharp knife (not stainless steel). The wood should be a smooth-grained variety. Take the wood in one hand and the knife in the other, and work with a series of tight, paring, thumb-pushing strokes (see Fig 23). The only way to become good at whittling is to get plenty of practice. In the first instance, try working with a piece of lime or basswood.

FIG 23

FIXING HINGES

The two most common hinge types are decorative brass hinges surface mounted with countersunk screws set flush with the hinge plate, and steel hinges set in a recess and fixed with countersunk steel screws. To recess a hinge, mark round the flap with the point of a fine-bladed knife, use a chisel to chop down to the waste side of the scored line, and finally skim out the waste with a sharp chisel. Work cautiously so that the hinge is a tight push-fit in the recess, and take care to control the chisel so that it doesn't lift the surrounding grain. If you are worried about recessing a hinge, either have several trial runs on scrap wood until you get it right, or opt for hinges that sit flush with the surface. There are a lot of different designs on the market, so you can easily choose a type that suits your needs and skill level. Always obtain screws at the same time as the hinges, to ensure that the countersink is compatible.

SANDING

The sanding or rubbing-down procedure involves using a variety of sandpapers to produce a smooth finish. Use the sandpaper as it is or fold it round a sanding block (see Fig 24), or use an electric sander (see Fig 25). It is a good idea to sand several times during a project – when the edges have been sawn, after the glue has cured, and before and after the final finish. Use ordinary glasspaper for the initial rubbing down, and fine-grade aluminium oxide paper when you want to achieve a special finish. Aluminium oxide paper is more expensive than glasspaper, but it lasts much longer. The best electric sander is an orbital type that is really good for large, flat surfaces. When you are sanding, work in a ventilated area and wear a dust mask (see page 11).

NATURAL FINISHES

A natural finish literally means that the wood is sanded and then left in its natural state, but the term has also come to mean a surface that has been oiled or waxed. Danish oil and teak oil can be applied with a lint-free cotton cloth or a brush (see Fig 26). You lay on a thin coat, let it dry, wipe it over with the finest grade of sandpaper to remove the "nibs" (the rough texture created by raised wood fibres that are left after the first coat of oil has soaked in) and then apply another thin coat. If you want to soften the surface, you can follow the second rubbing down with wax polish.

For projects that come into direct contact with food, replace teak or Danish oil with a vegetable oil. Ordinary olive oil wiped on with a cloth works well (see Fig 27).

FIG 24

FIG 26

FIG 25

FIG 27

PAINTED FINISHES

When it comes to painting a solid colour you have a choice between using spirit-based oil paint (see Fig 28) or water-based acrylic paint. Both paints need to be carefully applied with a brush. Though there is very little visual difference between the end results produced by the two types of paint, brushes used for oil paint need to be cleaned with white spirit, while those used for acrylic paint can be cleaned under running water. Choose paints for their depth and quality of colour, rather than for anything else. As for the side-effects of working with paint, you may find that oil fumes will make you woozy, while acrylic fumes will dry your throat. Whichever paint you are using, wear a mask to protect you from toxic vapours, and as far as possible, do the painting out in the open.

FIG 28

SPECIAL FINISHES

When using American oak, you can obtain an interesting finish by scouring the grain with a wire brush. A wire-brushed finish has a nice feel, and the rugged surface means that you don't have to worry about pets' paws damaging it. The wire brush is rubbed in the direction of the grain (see Fig 29) until the soft areas break down, and the wood is finished with oil.

The candle-smoking technique is fun to do and perfect for covering up a poor-grade wood. Brush the painted surface with oil-based varnish, wait for it to become tacky, and then play the candle flame over the surface (see Fig 30). Always wait for the surface to go tacky (so that it just takes a fingerprint), and always keep the can of varnish and the brushes well away from the candle. This is a procedure that is best managed with a friend's help, in an area well away from the workshop. Practise on an offcut before you start.

FIG 29

FIG 30

KEY TO THE PROJECTS

Ideal beginner's project

Perfect for those who have some experience of woodworking

Ambitious projects, which experienced carpenters will enjoy

Tableware

We all enjoy sitting around a table and sharing a meal with family and friends. But just think how much more fun it would be if you could boast that you had made the tableware. This project involves making two items: oak eggcups that double up as napkin rings, and heart-shaped plywood table mats with their own rack. The designs are somewhat kitsch, but the fact that the shapes and the colours are over the top is part of their appeal, and children will love them too. Also, both eggcups and mats are very practical, and perfect for a young family.

The woodworking techniques are amazingly easy – just a case of drilling large holes and fretting the plywood on the scroll saw. The painting is slightly more difficult and needs to be done with care. When the project is finished, and the items are being used at the breakfast table, don't be surprised to see your children piling the eggcups into stacks and playing with the heart shapes – take it as a sign that they are a success!

Essential Tools

workbench with vice and holdfast, compasses, pencil, rule, square, bench drill press or electric drill, 45 mm forstner bit, clamps, sanding block, 25 mm and 10 mm paintbrushes, scissors, scroll saw, router and router table, 5 mm radius cutter, 5 mm and 8 mm twist bits, pilot-countersink bit, medium-size hammer

OTHER USEFUL TOOLS
cordless screwdriver, power sander, dividers, marking knife

Tableware

You'll need to know

DRILLING HOLES
p.17

ROUTING EDGE PROFILES
p.21

CUTTING CURVED SHAPES
p.16

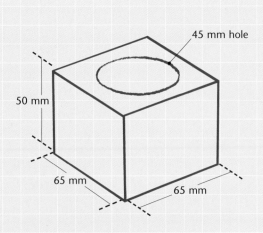

45 mm hole

50 mm

65 mm

65 mm

Materials

oak and plywood (see cutting list)

sandpaper grades 80 and 120

acrylic paint: four colours to suit

clear spirit-based gloss varnish

thin paper and card

2 x 70 mm lengths 8 mm dowel

PVA glue

gloss paint: bright red

white spirit to clean the brushes

Cutting List

6 pieces oak 65 x 65 x 50 mm (eggcup blocks)

1 piece plywood 260 x 250 x 12 mm
(heart rack back board)

1 piece plywood 220 x 210 x 12 mm
(heart rack front board)

6 pieces plywood 220 x 210 x 6 mm
(heart mats)

This eggcup/napkin ring design relies on the block of wood being in perfect condition – there must be absolutely no splits running into the end grain.

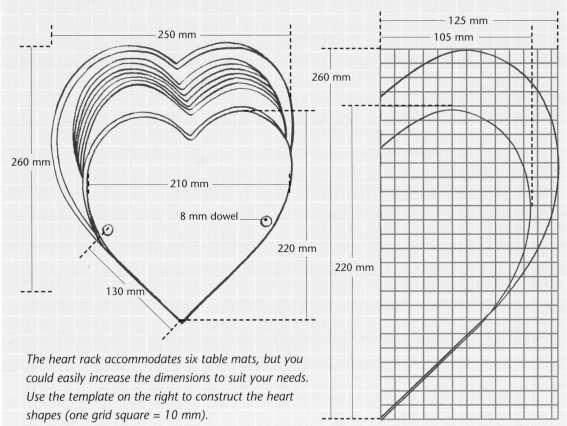

250 mm

260 mm

210 mm

8 mm dowel

220 mm

130 mm

125 mm

105 mm

260 mm

220 mm

The heart rack accommodates six table mats, but you could easily increase the dimensions to suit your needs. Use the template on the right to construct the heart shapes (one grid square = 10 mm).

EGGCUPS/NAPKIN RINGS

FIG 1

1 Take your prepared oak blocks and check them over to make sure that they are free from cracks. Draw crossed diagonals to establish the position of the centre points (see Fig 1). Do this on both sides of the block.

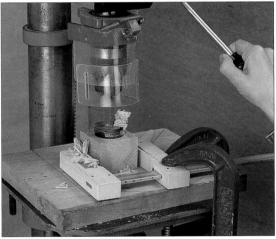

FIG 2

2 Fit the 45 mm forstner bit in the bench drill press. Secure the workpiece with clamps – one to grip the workpiece, another to hold the waste board down on the table, and another clamp to hold the gripping clamp. Run a hole through the 50 mm thickness (see Fig 2). Keep clearing the waste so the bit does not overheat.

TIP

The only way of drilling a smooth-sided, large-diameter hole is to use a forstner bit. They are much more expensive than ordinary bits, but they will last a lot longer. When you bore out the holes, run the bit in little by little, so the waste is removed without overheating the bit.

FIG 3

3 Use the graded sandpapers to rub down all the surfaces to a smooth finish. When you are happy with the results, wipe away the mess and move to a clean, dust-free area that you have set aside for painting. Take one block at a time and brush on the acrylic colours – make one side red, another side blue, and so on (see Fig 3). Continue until all the sides of all of the blocks are painted. When the paint is completely dry, use the finest grade of sandpaper to gently rub down the raised hairs of wood. Finally, give all the surfaces a coat of clear gloss varnish.

HEART TABLE MATS

FIG 4

4 Draw the two heart shapes on paper and then transfer to card. Use the card template to draw out the shapes on the plywood (see Fig 4). Mark the shape with a single drawn line, so there is no doubting the line of cut.

FIG 6

6 Attach the router to its table and fit the radius cutter. Set the boards face down on the table and profile the edges so they are nicely rounded (see Fig 6). Do both sides of the heart front and back board that make the rack.

FIG 5

5 Cut out the eight hearts on the scroll saw – two from the 12 mm plywood, and six from the 6 mm. Run a cut straight in and out of the cleft at the top of the heart, and then work from the point back into the cleft (see Fig 6). Saw at a steady, easy pace, all the while making sure that the cut is to the waste side of the drawn line.

FIG 7

7 Draw in the position of the dowel centres on the hearts for the rack. Drill a pair of holes in the front board with the 8 mm twist bit. Hold the two boards together with a length of dowel, and drill the other holes (see Fig 7). Drill out the two hanging holes with the 5 mm twist bit and finish with the pilot-countersink bit.

FIG 8

FIG 9

8 Take the two 70 mm dowels and round over the ends with sandpaper. Set the back and front boards together on the dowels and fix them in place with glue. Use the hammer to nudge the boards about 38 mm apart, so that the dowel ends protrude on the front face (see Fig 8), and wipe away the glue. Check to make sure that the rack holds all six mats comfortably.

9 Wipe away all traces of dust and move to a clean area that you have set aside for painting. Give all surfaces a couple of coats of bright red gloss paint (see Fig 9), so that the hearts look attractively shiny. Finally, when the paint is absolutely dry, rub over the surfaces with the finest grade of sandpaper and give everything a coat of varnish. Sand and varnish again.

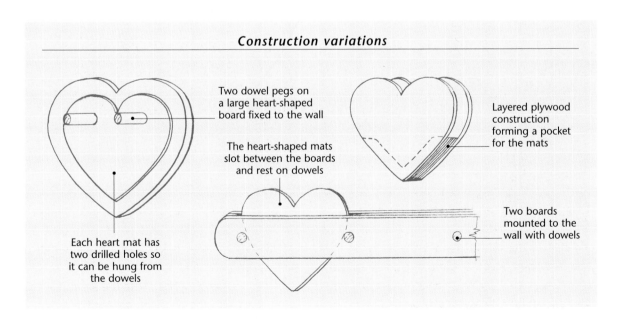

Construction variations

Two dowel pegs on a large heart-shaped board fixed to the wall

The heart-shaped mats slot between the boards and rest on dowels

Each heart mat has two drilled holes so it can be hung from the dowels

Layered plywood construction forming a pocket for the mats

Two boards mounted to the wall with dowels

Kitchen wall rack

The wall rack is a great project for the kitchen. If you have got nowhere to hang your pots and pans, and spoons, slices and spatulas are strewn across the worksurface, transform your life with this really attractive design feature, which stores all the utensils at an easy-to-reach height. And if you are keen on drying herbs, or collecting and displaying antique utensils, the holes at the ends of the slats and the brass cuphooks will come in extremely useful for suspending items, using ribbons if necessary.

The wall rack is very easy to to make – involving just a small amount of work on the scroll saw, and a bit of drilling. The success of the project relies on the spacing of the slats, which has to be just right, and the finish – you do need to take time with the sanding. The good thing about the design of the rack is its flexibility. For example, if you require a wider rack, all you do is add another vertical runner and lengthen the slats accordingly. Measure the wall space and adjust the overall size of the rack to fit. Check the position of water pipes and power cables before you screw the rack to the wall.

Essential Tools

workbench with vice and holdfast, compasses, pencil, rule, square, clamp, scroll saw, bench drill press, 10 mm, 5 mm and 3 mm twist bits, electric drill, screwdriver, sanding block, paintbrush

OTHER USEFUL TOOLS
cordless screwdriver, power sander, marking knife, block plane

Kitchen wall rack

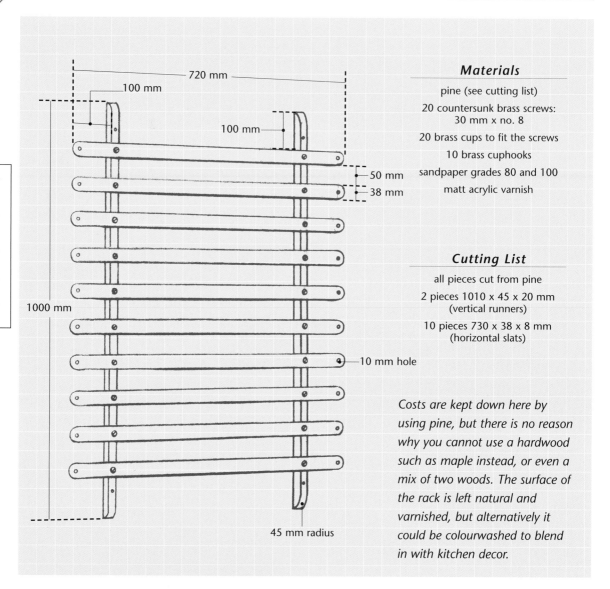

720 mm

100 mm

100 mm

50 mm

38 mm

1000 mm

10 mm hole

45 mm radius

Materials

pine (see cutting list)

20 countersunk brass screws:
30 mm x no. 8

20 brass cups to fit the screws

10 brass cuphooks

sandpaper grades 80 and 100

matt acrylic varnish

Cutting List

all pieces cut from pine

2 pieces 1010 x 45 x 20 mm
(vertical runners)

10 pieces 730 x 38 x 8 mm
(horizontal slats)

*Costs are kept down here by
using pine, but there is no reason
why you cannot use a hardwood
such as maple instead, or even a
mix of two woods. The surface of
the rack is left natural and
varnished, but alternatively it
could be colourwashed to blend
in with kitchen decor.*

**You'll need
to know**

**CUTTING CURVED
SHAPES**
p.16

DRILLING HOLES
p.17

SCREWING
p.22

FIG 1

1 Check the prepared wood for possible problems such as splits and badly placed knots. While the runners can have a few knots here and there, it is most important that the slats are smooth grained along their length. If you have doubts about the quality of your wood, look for better stock. Take the two 1010 mm runners, set the compasses to 45 mm and draw quarter-circle curves 5 mm short of the ends. Use the scroll saw to cut the ends to shape (see Fig 1).

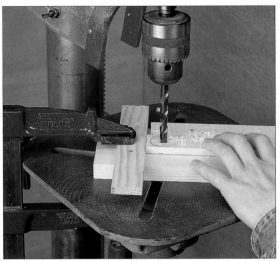

FIG 2

TIP

The trickiest part of this project is getting the whole thing true, so that the slats are horizontal to each other and square with the runners. The best way to do this is to set out the dimensions on one runner (the width of the slats and the spacing) and then to clamp the two runners side by side and run the lines across with the square. This way of working ensures that both pieces of wood are set out with an identical pattern of guidelines.

2 Take the slats and use the compasses to set out circles 35 mm in diameter on the ends. Have the circles set back 5 mm from the ends, so that the slats all finish up at 720 mm long. On the bench drill press, run 10 mm holes through the centre points (see Fig 2).

FIG 3

FIG 4

3 Cut the ends of the slats to shape on the scroll saw (see Fig 3). Do your best to cut slightly to the waste side of the drawn line, so that the curve is true. If you fit a new blade and work at an easy pace, the sawn edges will hardly need sanding. Make sure the blade is fitted so the teeth point down towards the table.

4 Mark guidelines on the runners, spacing the slats 50 mm apart. For each screw, drill 5 mm holes through the slats and 3 mm pilot holes into the runners. Fix the slats with the screws and cups (see Fig 4). Sand all the surfaces, fit the cuphooks, and varnish the whole wall rack. The end grain might need a couple of coats.

Tea tray

The styles of the 1950s do not excite everyone, but there is something about the simplicity of the period that is most appealing. Designers of the time experimented with smooth curves, new materials such as plastics, and lots of primary colours, making many of the household items appear quite daring. This little 1950s-style tray is also quite different to the ornate mahogany and brass of earlier times, instead using a sheet of plywood with simple strip wood handles. White and red enamel paint – which would have been just right for the red-and-white kitchens of the 1950s – are used here, but you may prefer to select an alternative colour scheme.

The making procedures are very easy. All the parts are fretted out on the scroll saw, the individual components are painted, and then the tray is put together with brass screws. What could be easier? That said, the success of the project relies on the sawn lines being crisp and clean, and the paint finish being smooth and free from runs and dribbles. If you have doubts about your painting skills, practise on a piece of scrap wood first.

Essential Tools

workbench with vice, compasses, pencil, rule, square, scroll saw, sanding block, paintbrush, electric drill, 3 mm twist bit, pilot-countersink bit, screwdriver

OTHER USEFUL TOOLS
cordless screwdriver, power sander, dividers, marking knife, block plane

Tea tray

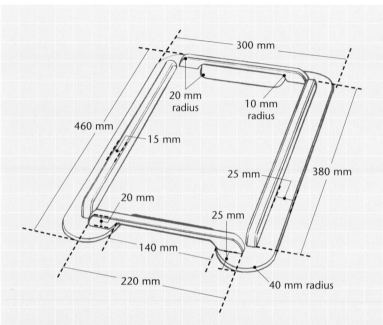

300 mm

20 mm radius

10 mm radius

460 mm

15 mm

25 mm

380 mm

20 mm

25 mm

140 mm

40 mm radius

220 mm

Materials

plywood and pine (see cutting list)

sandpaper grade 100

gloss paint: red and white

white spirit to clean the brush

12 countersunk brass screws:
15 mm x no. 8

Cutting List

1 piece of plywood
460 x 300 x 6 mm
(base board)

2 pieces of pine
380 x 20 x 15 mm
(side strips)

2 pieces of pine
220 x 20 x 15 mm
(handle strips)

If you make the tray larger, increase the dimensions of the handle strips so that they are strong enough to carry a heavier weight.

You'll need to know

CUTTING CURVED SHAPES
p.16

PAINTED FINISHES
p.25

SCREWING
p.22

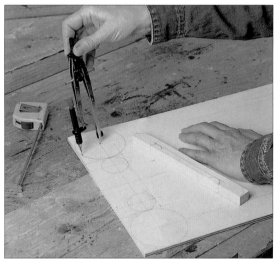

FIG 1

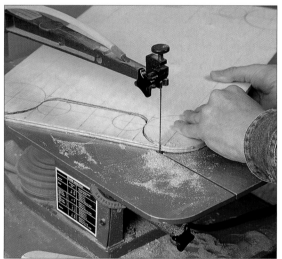

FIG 2

1 Measure 40 mm along from each end of the base board, rule a line across and draw the large circles (40 mm radius) and the smaller circles (20 mm radius). Set out the handles with radii of 10 mm and 20 mm (see Fig 1).

2 Check against the working drawing to ensure that all is correct, and then fret out the parts on the scroll saw (base, handles and side strips). The line of cut must be slightly to the waste side of the drawn line (see Fig 2).

TIPS

The painting is tricky – to achieve a good finish, lay the paint on as two or more thin coats. Wipe away the dust, lay on the first coat and let it dry, sand slightly, lay on another coat, and so on until you have a high-shine finish.

4 Mark out the position of the side and handle strips on the base board and drill 3 mm pilot holes through the base and about 5 mm into the strips. Countersink the base holes on what will be the underside of the tray, and finally screw the strips in place (see Fig 4).

FIG 3

3 Sand the sawn faces to a slightly round-edged finish. Paint the parts with the gloss paint – red for the side and handle strips and white for both sides of the base. When the paint is completely dry, repeat the rubbing down with the finest grade of sandpaper (see Fig 3), and lay on another thin coat of paint.

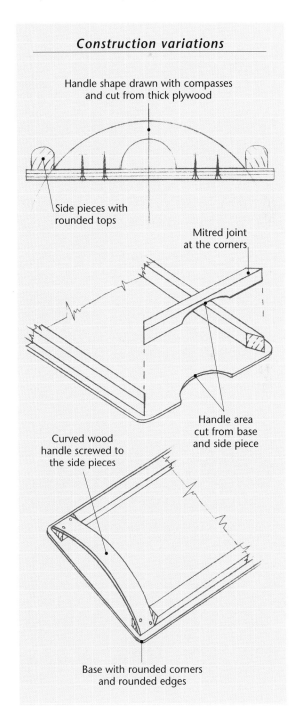

Construction variations

Handle shape drawn with compasses and cut from thick plywood

Side pieces with rounded tops

Mitred joint at the corners

Handle area cut from base and side piece

Curved wood handle screwed to the side pieces

Base with rounded corners and rounded edges

FIG 4

Consul shelf

This project looks to the painted folk art woodwork that was made in America in the nineteenth century by the German settlers in Pennsylvania. It was characterized by very simple construction, using lots of nails, and was painted either with brightly coloured motifs and designs, or given an overall texture to fool the eye into believing that it was made from an exotic wood.

This particular little shelf is decorated by a technique known as candle marbling or smoking. The wood is painted with a base colour, usually red, blue or green, and then, when the paint is dry, the surface is brushed with spirit-based varnish, left until it is tacky, and finally the tip of the flame of a lighted candle is played over the surface. The black carbon from the flame bleeds into the varnish to create a shimmering, opalescent blue-black effect, a bit like the bloom on a fresh black plum.

The shelf's construction is very basic. The three components are fretted out on the scroll saw and then simply fixed with screws that run down from the top and in from the back. The only slightly more ornate piece of woodwork is the cyma curve bracket that supports the shelf.

Essential Tools

workbench with vice, compass, pencil, rule, square, scroll saw, router and router table, 6.3 mm radius cutter, sanding block, hand drill, 3 mm twist bit, pilot-countersink bit, screwdriver, 2 paintbrushes

OTHER USEFUL TOOLS
cordless screwdriver, power sander, electric drill, dividers, marking knife, block plane, tenon saw

Consul shelf

300 mm

150 mm radius

135 mm radius

270 mm

The consul shelf is screwed together:
2 screws fix the back to the bracket,
3 screws fix the shelf to the back and
1 screw fixes the shelf to the bracket.
Below: template for the bracket.

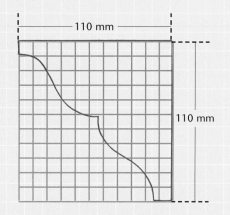

110 mm

110 mm

Materials

pine (see cutting list)
sandpaper grades 80 and 150
6 countersunk steel screws: 30 mm x no. 8
matt, spirit-based tile paint: red
spirit-based clear varnish
white spirit to clean the brushes
large candle

Cutting List

all pieces cut from pine
1 piece 300 x 160 x 18 mm (shelf board)
1 piece 270 x 140 x 18 mm (back board)
1 piece 110 x 110 x 18 mm (bracket board)

FIG 1

1 Use the compasses to set out the shelf board at a radius of 150 mm, and the back board at 135 mm. Transfer the shape of the cyma curve to the bracket board (see Fig 1).

FIG 2

2 Fret out the three component parts on the scroll saw – the half-circle of the shelf board to a finished diameter of 150 mm, the half-circle back board to a diameter of 270 mm, and the right-angled cyma-curve bracket to measure 110 mm x 110 mm (see Fig 2).

FIG 3

3 Fit the radius cutter in the router and attach the router to its table. Cut radius curves on the underside of the shelf and on the front of the back board (see Fig 3).

FIG 4

4 Use the sanding block and fine-grade sand-paper to rub down everything to a smooth finish. Pay particular attention to the edge of the shelf and the sawn edges of the cyma curve (see Fig 4). Drill 3 mm pilot holes for the screws and countersink with the pilot-countersink bit.

FIG 5

5 Have a trial fitting to make sure that every-thing is correct, and then screw the pieces together. The screws run through the back board into the bracket, and through the shelf board into the top edge of the back board and into the bracket (see Fig 5).

FIG 6

6 Paint the shelf red. When the paint is dry, lay on a thin coat of varnish. When the var-nish is tacky and almost dry, light the candle and play the tip of the flame over the surface to create the marbled effect (see Fig 6). Be careful not to overdo the smoking, especially at the edges, or it will obliterate the red colour. Finally, give the shelf a second coat of varnish.

TIP

Caution – keep the varnish and white spirit away from the lighted candle, because both are highly flammable. The varnished surface must be tacky before you start the candle work, or you won't achieve the correct result.

Colonial wall shelf

The houses of early settlers in America were filled with all manner of shelves. There were consul shelves for candles, shelves for bags and pouches, shelves for storing dry goods, and so on. All were put together with the minimum of joints, and charmingly decorated in a naïve style. The shelf in this project beautifully recreates the work of the New England craftsmen, who were masters of compass work and the cyma curve.

The low-tech housing groove and glued construction make the shelf a great project for beginners who have a relatively limited tool kit. Pine is used throughout, making it economical to build. The highly fretted edges turn it into a very decorative piece, so it would be perfect for a living room display shelf. The side boards are cleverly designed so that the symmetrical shapes are easy to achieve by eye and with compasses. All you do is draw the design on one side of the centre-line and then trace it off and flip it over to the other side. Make sure that the fretted edges of the side boards are free from knots and splits, especially the curves lying just in front of the shelves.

Essential Tools

workbench with vice and holdfast, compasses,
pencil, rule, square, scroll saw, router and router table,
13 mm groove cutter, clamps, knife, sanding block,
paintbrush, screwdriver

OTHER USEFUL TOOLS
cordless screwdriver, power sander, marking knife,
block plane

Colonial wall shelf

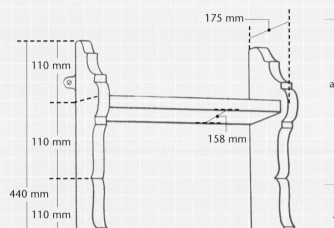

175 mm

110 mm

110 mm

158 mm

440 mm

110 mm

110 mm

17 mm

316 mm

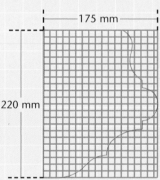

Materials

pine (see cutting list)

PVA glue

sandpaper grades 80 and 150

artist's oil paint: red, burnt umber and black

teak oil

white spirit to clean the brush

4 x 30 mm brass mirror hangers
with brass screws to fit

Cutting List

all pieces cut from pine

2 pieces 440 x 175 x 18 mm (side boards)

2 pieces 300 x 158 x 18 mm (shelves)

175 mm

220 mm

You could conceal the mirror hangers by placing them on the inside, but traditonally hangers were set as "ears", so they become a decorative detail, and we have followed suit here.

You'll need to know

CUTTING CURVED SHAPES
p.16

ROUTING A HOUSING GROOVE
p.20

ROUTING A REBATE
p.20

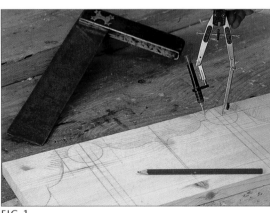

FIG 1

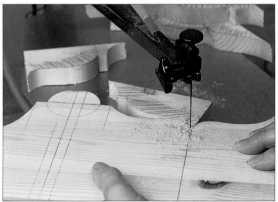

FIG 2

1 Arrange the two 440 mm sides so that the best edges are facing outwards. Divide into four equal pieces and use the square, rule and compasses to set out the design (see Fig 1).

2 Using the scroll saw, run a cut along the centre-line, and then back out of the kerf (saw cut). Fret out the design, finishing in the cleft (see Fig 2). Do this for both side boards.

FIG 3

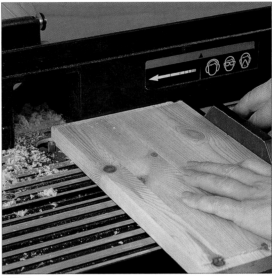

FIG 4

3 Use the router and 13 mm groove cutter to cut the housing grooves. Clamp a side board to the bench, and with waste strips in place, adjust the position of the guide to ensure that the router bit is perfectly on course. Set the depth guide to 10 mm. Finally, switch on the power, hold the router base plate hard up against the guide strip, check that the flex is clear, and cut the housing groove (see Fig 3).

4 Mount the router on the router table. Set the fence to 10 mm, and cut shoulders on the shelf ends (see Fig 4). Use the knife to whittle the shoulders to fit the stopped ends of the housing grooves. Glue and clamp up. Sand to a smooth finish. Mix a little of the red, black and burnt umber paint into the teak oil, and brush on one or more coats. Screw the mirror hangers to the back edges of the side boards.

Construction variations

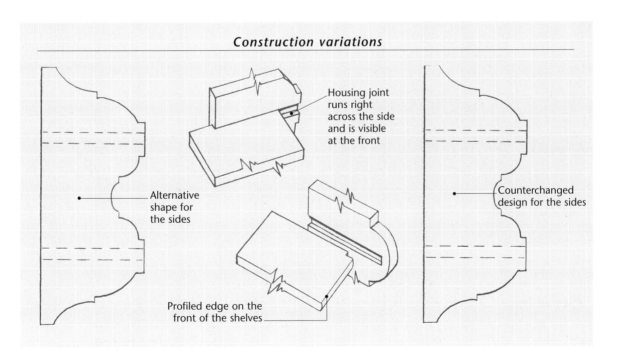

Alternative shape for the sides

Housing joint runs right across the side and is visible at the front

Profiled edge on the front of the shelves

Counterchanged design for the sides

Arts and Crafts mirror

The design of this mirror pays homage to Arts and Crafts designers such as Gustav Stickley and Ernest Gimson with its use of proportion, very slender through-tenons, the way the horizontal members extend beyond the limits of the frame, and the use of dowels to hold the joints together. However, although an Arts and Crafts form will happily blend into most homes, an altogether lighter feel – both in colour and proportions – is perhaps more consistent with modern styles. So, instead of using thick-section oak, a much thinner section of straight-grained pine is used here.

Made from pine throughout, with dowels standing proud and the back rebated to take the mirror glass, this is quite a challenging project. The tricky part is cutting the mortises through the thickness of the wood: you will be cutting a mortise 8 mm wide through a 20 mm piece of pine, with only a 6 mm thickness of wood at either side of the mortise. It will test your skills! If you are not sure whether your woodworking expertise or your tools are up to it, have a trial run on scrap wood beforehand.

Essential Tools

workbench with vice and holdfast, compasses, pencil, rule, square, mortise gauge, clamps, bench drill press, 6 mm and 12 mm forstner bits, mallet, 6 mm and 20 mm bevel-edge chisels, marking knife, router and router table, penknife, 10 mm groove cutter, block plane, small hammer, sanding block, screwdriver

OTHER USEFUL TOOLS
power sander

Arts and Crafts mirror

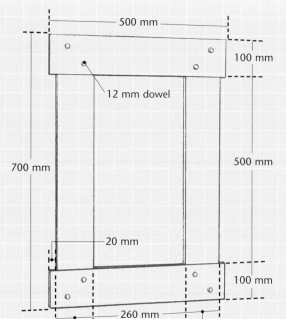

500 mm

100 mm

12 mm dowel

700 mm

500 mm

20 mm

100 mm

260 mm

100 mm

100 mm

Materials

pine (see cutting list)

PVA glue

sandpaper grades 80 and 150

beeswax polish and lint-free cotton cloth

mirror glass 520 x 280 x 5 mm

6 mirror clips with screws to fit

2 brass screw eyes and brass picture wire: size and design to suit

Cutting List

all pieces cut from pine

2 pieces 700 x 100 x 20 mm (long sides)

2 pieces 500 x 100 x 20 mm (short sides)

8 x 25 mm lengths of 12 mm pine dowel

If you make the frame bigger, you will also need to increase the width and thickness of the wood.

FIG 1

FIG 2

1 Take the two 500 mm lengths of wood and use the square to position the mortises 20 mm along from the ends. Set the spurs of the mortise gauge to 8 mm apart, and score the lines so that they are centred on the 20 mm thickness of wood (see Fig 1). Do this on opposite edges, and on both ends of the wood.

2 Bore through all the mortises with the bench drill press and 6 mm bit, and then use the mallet and bevel-edge chisels to pare the mortises to a smooth, true finish (see Fig 2). Work from both sides of the mortise to keep the edges clean. Don't damage the ends of the holes by levering the tool against the wood.

FIG 3

3 Use the square, marking knife and gauge to set out the 100 mm-long tenons. Attach the router to its table, fit the 10 mm groove cutter in the router, set the fence to 100 mm and the depth of cut to 6 mm. Make a series of passes to cut away the waste (see Fig 3). Re-run this procedure on both sides and both ends, so that you finish up with 8 mm-thick tenons.

FIG 4

4 Reset the fence to 10 mm and run the rebates for the mirror on the inside back edges of the frame. Put the frame components together and use the 12 mm bit to bore the dowel holes through the joints. Check for squareness and overall good fit (see Fig 4), and use the block plane to tidy up the end grain.

FIG 5

5 Fit the frame together, dribble glue in the drilled holes, and tap the dowels home with the hammer (see Fig 5). Leave the dowels standing proud on the front face of the frame. When the glue is completely dry, use the chisel to remove any runs and to trim the edges of the dowels to a slightly round-edged finish. Check that all rebated corners are free from blobs of glue. Use the graded sandpapers to rub the frame to a smooth finish. Finally, wipe away the dust, burnish the frame with the beeswax, fit the mirror glass and screw in the clips to hold it in place, and fix the screw eyes and the hanging wire.

TIP

To be certain that the mirror glass will fit the frame really well, it is best to take the frame to a glazier so it can be measured and the glass cut to fit exactly. Make sure that the glass is properly wrapped and protected before you take it away.

Studio shelf system

This project covers that most basic of items – a simple shelf. For ease of making, it takes a bit of beating – there are no joints to cut, it is just made up of six planks and a handful of screws and dowels. The design is so well considered and cheap to make that you could easily put together a batch of units. As the shelves are fixed directly to the wall with screws through the back boards, they can be removed easily and taken with you when you move house. Simple to make and trouble-free to fit – the perfect shelves!

Made of pine throughout, the construction is wonderfully straightforward. Instead of having the screws running into the end grain (which technically is a bad idea because the threads tend to pull out), they run down through pilot holes and into dowels set across the grain. The dowels are stained black, and the screwheads are covered with glued plugs. When you are driving the screws home, be careful not to over-tighten them to the extent that you expand the dowels and split the wood. Arrange the dowels so that the grain runs at right angles to the screw.

Essential Tools

workbench with vice and holdfast, compasses, pencil, rule, square, block plane, hammer, clamps, bench drill press, 12 mm twist bit, large bevel-edge knife, 7 mm counter-bore bit with a plug cutter to match, screwdriver, sanding block, paintbrush

OTHER USEFUL TOOLS
cordless screwdriver, power sander, marking knife

Studio shelf system

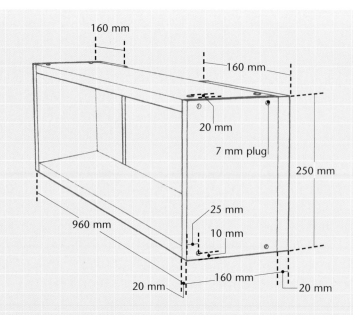

If you like the design of the shelf system but would prefer not to use dowels, see the Adjustable porch chair on page 128 for an alternative method of fixing, using hex-head fasteners.

Dimensions shown: 160 mm, 160 mm, 20 mm, 7 mm plug, 250 mm, 25 mm, 10 mm, 960 mm, 20 mm, 160 mm, 20 mm

Materials

pine (see cutting list)

wood offcuts for the drilling jig

6 nails for the jig: size to suit

200 mm length of 12 mm dowel

22 countersunk steel screws:
30 mm x no. 8

sandpaper grades 150 to 300

black felt-tip spirit marker

PVA glue

spirit-based matt varnish

white spirit to clean brush

Cutting List

all pieces cut from pine

2 pieces 960 x 160 x 20 mm
(shelf boards)

2 pieces 250 x 160 x 20 mm
(end boards)

2 pieces 250 x 160 x 20 mm
(back boards)

You'll need to know

HAND PLANING
p.18

DRILLING HOLES
p.17

SCREWING
p.22

FIG 1

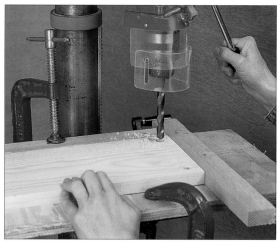

FIG 2

1 Take all six prepared boards (cut to size and planed) and check them over to make sure that they are in good condition, with no warps, splits or badly placed knots. Use the block plane to bring the ends to a good finish and to bevel all the edges slightly (see Fig 1).

2 Use the hammer, nails and offcuts to build a jig (a device for holding a component during construction) to contain one end of a shelf board. Put a shelf in the jig and clamp it to the table of the bench drill press so the 12 mm bit is in position. Bore out the dowel holes (see Fig 2).

FIG 3

3 Use a rule and pencil to mark off 23 mm intervals on the 12 mm dowel. Set the knife on the mark, and roll the dowel to cut it through (see Fig 3). Note how the wide bevel on the knife gives the dowel a rounded end.

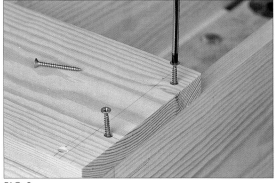

FIG 5

5 Use the counter-bore bit to drill holes through the end boards and back boards. Drive the screws home so that their heads are about 5 mm below the surface (see Fig 5 – shows back board being screwed to shelf).

FIG 4

4 Sand the dowel ends to a slightly domed finish. Stain the ends with the felt-tip (see Fig 4). Push the dowels into the holes in the ends of the shelves (they will stand slightly proud).

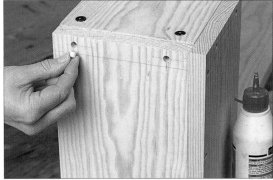

FIG 6

6 Cut plugs from a scrap of pine and glue them in place to cover the screws. Finally, sand the entire shelf system to a good finish and brush on a coat of varnish (see Fig 6).

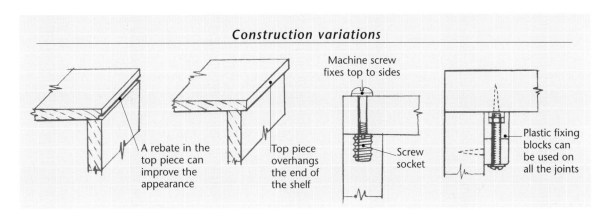

Construction variations

A rebate in the top piece can improve the appearance

Top piece overhangs the end of the shelf

Machine screw fixes top to sides

Screw socket

Plastic fixing blocks can be used on all the joints

Waste bin

This is the perfect bin for the design-conscious home. Get rid of your creaky woven baskets and plastic tubs left over from the 1970s – now you can have a bin that looks as if it belongs in the twenty-first century. This bin will also look good in a home office, or perhaps in the children's room.

Made of top-quality birch plywood throughout, this is one of the easiest projects in the book. The holes must be cut very carefully, and the five boards need to be prepared, glued and pinned together, but apart from that, the construction is amazingly straightforward. The design is also very flexible, so you can choose to change the pattern of drilled holes, or go for a fretted design rather than have holes, or paint the bin in a bright primary colour instead of the natural finish. Do not be tempted to cut costs by using one of the soft-centred plywoods (those originating from Malaysia), because they are of inferior quality. You must use best-quality birch plywood. Ask your supplier for advice if you are not sure what to buy.

—————— Essential Tools ——————

workbench with vice, pencil, rule, square, awl,
bench drill press, 25 mm and 40 mm forstner bits,
clamps, power sander, pin hammer, sanding block,
paintbrush

OTHER USEFUL TOOLS
marking knife

Waste bin

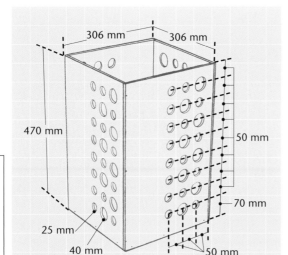

306 mm   306 mm

470 mm

50 mm

70 mm

25 mm

40 mm   50 mm

Note the way the sides follow each other so that you only see one edge on each side.

Materials

birch plywood (see cutting list)

masking tape

sandpaper grades 100 and 150

PVA glue

24 x 12 mm steel pins

teak oil

Cutting List

all pieces cut from birch plywood

4 pieces 470 x 300 x 6 mm (sides)

1 piece 294 x 294 x 12 mm (base)

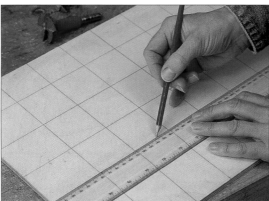

FIG 1

You'll need to know

DRILLING HOLES
p.17

SANDING
p.24

NAILING AND PINNING
p.22

1 Take one of the side boards and use the rule and square to draw out a 50 x 50 mm grid (see Fig 1). Double-check the measurements to make sure that the grid is accurate.

FIG 2

2 Take the four boards that make up the sides and sandwich them together, with the gridded board on top of the stack. Strap them up with masking tape (see Fig 2). Study the design, decide on the pattern of holes you want, and spike in the centre points with the awl.

FIG 3

3 Fit one or other of the forstner bits in the bench drill press, put a waste board on the drill table, and set to work boring the pattern of holes (see Fig 3). To ensure that each hole is cleanly worked, centre the bit on the spiked point, and then clamp the workpiece in place.

FIG 4

4 When you have bored all the holes, remove the masking tape, and use the sander to rub down the surfaces to a smooth finish (see Fig 4). Be careful not to blur the edges.

FIG 5

5 Fold a piece of fine-grade sandpaper and use it to wipe round the cut edges of the drilled holes (see Fig 5). Continue until the edges are smooth to the touch.

FIG 6

6 Sand down the edges of the base board and glue and pin the sides in place (see Fig 6). Don't let the pins run off course and split the plywood. Finally, sand the bin to a smooth finish and wipe on a coat of teak oil.

TIP

If you are worried about your ability to knock the pins into the edge of the thin plywood, then either ask a friend to help you align the pins, or drill pilot holes with a hand drill and a fine bit.

Construction variations

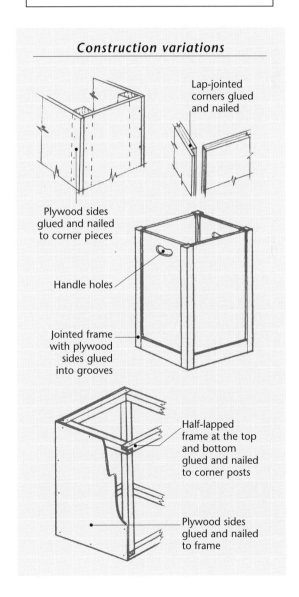

Lap-jointed corners glued and nailed

Plywood sides glued and nailed to corner pieces

Handle holes

Jointed frame with plywood sides glued into grooves

Half-lapped frame at the top and bottom glued and nailed to corner posts

Plywood sides glued and nailed to frame

Child's stool

This beautiful, country-style stool fulfils a number of roles. It works well as a footstool, for standing on to reach cupboards and also as a child's special seat.

Even if you are the newest of new carpenters, you will be able to manage the construction process easily. Made from 20 mm-thick pine boards throughout, the components are fretted out on the scroll saw. The splayed legs are housed in grooves cut on the inside face of the two apron boards, and the stool is held together with screws. This stool is painted yellow, but other bright colours, including fire-engine red and electric blue, also look attractive. You could also paint each part in a different colour.

Essential Tools

workbench with vice and holdfast, compasses,
pencil, rule, square, bevel gauge, scroll saw, bench drill
press or electric drill, 10 mm and 5 mm twist bits,
tenon saw, 16 mm bevel-edge chisel, block plane,
sanding block, pilot-countersink bit,
screwdriver, paintbrush

OTHER USEFUL TOOLS
cordless screwdriver, power sander, dividers,
marking knife

Child's stool

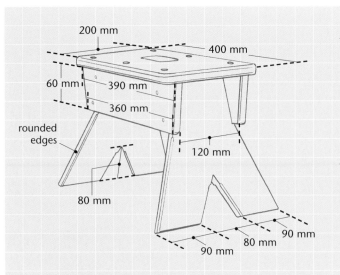

200 mm
400 mm
60 mm
390 mm
360 mm
rounded edges
120 mm
80 mm
90 mm
80 mm
90 mm

Materials

pine (see cutting list)
sandpaper grades 80 and 150
12 countersunk steel screws: 30 mm x no. 8
gloss paint: yellow
white spirit to clean the brush

Cutting List

all pieces cut from pine
1 piece 400 x 200 x 18 mm (seat board)
2 pieces 390 x 60 x 18 mm (apron boards)
2 pieces 260 x 260 x 18 mm (leg boards)

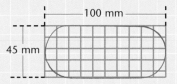

100 mm
45 mm

The hole in the centre of the seat (detail shown right), which doubles as a handle, must be large enough to ensure that a child cannot get a leg stuck in it.

You'll need to know

CUTTING CURVED SHAPES
p.16

HAND PLANING
p.18

PAINTED FINISHES
p.25

FIG 1

FIG 2

1 Check the prepared boards for possible problems such as splits and badly placed knots. Use the square and bevel gauge to carefully set out the design. When you come to the leg boards, start by drawing a centre-line, and then use the line as a reference point for all the subsequent measurements (see Fig 1).

2 Use the scroll saw to cut out the component parts. Work at a steady, controlled pace, making sure that the line of cut is slightly to the waste side of the drawn line (see Fig 2). If you feel the blade running off course, or it sags, or the cut edge of the wood goes brown and shiny, the blade probably needs replacing.

FIG 3

3 Drill a pilot hole through the seat with the 10 mm twist bit, pass one end of the scroll saw blade through the hole, refit the blade and tension it until it "pings". Cut along the marked line until the waste drops clear (see Fig 3).

TIP

When using a chisel to cut a housing groove, make sure that the chisel is slightly narrower than the finished width of the groove.

FIG 4

4 To create the housing groove on the apron boards, make two cuts with the tenon saw (at 20 mm from the end, slanting to 60 mm from the end; with a parallel 18 mm away, 5 mm deep). Clear the waste with the chisel (see Fig 4).

FIG 5

5 Use the block plane to work all the on-view edges to a slightly rounded finish (as shown in Figs 4 and 6). With the chisel and sandpaper, adjust the sides of the leg boards so that they meet the apron boards for a tight push-fit (see Fig 5). Pencil-label the parts so that the joints are cut to a paired fit.

FIG 6

6 Drill pilot holes with the 5 mm bit, followed by the pilot-countersink bit. Screw the apron boards to the legs and the seat board to the top edge of the aprons, countersinking all the screws. Rub down with the finest grade of sandpaper, wipe up all the dust, and give the stool a coat of yellow gloss paint (see Fig 6). Re-run the procedure for a high-shine finish.

Turned fruit bowl

Fruit always makes an attractive display while it is waiting to be eaten, particularly when it is contained in a beautiful bowl. Wooden bowls look especially appealing, and as a natural material, they complement the fruit perfectly. And what could be better than using a fruit bowl that you have made yourself? Just think of the kudos when your family and friends see the evidence of your talents – you can expect some orders for gifts.

There is no need to get involved in the expensive and wearisome business of searching around for a suitable lump of wood. The good thing about this project is that the bowl is made from straight-grained American oak, and the blank (form for the bowl) is built up in laminated slices cut from a prepared board. The laminating procedure is a bit messy and time-consuming, but on the other hand it means that you do not have to worry about loose knots or splits, or the wood warping out of shape.

────── Essential Tools ──────

workbench with vice, compasses, pencil, rule,
scroll saw, 4 long-reach sash or G-clamps, good-size
lathe with a 150 mm-diameter face plate and the
capacity to turn a blank bigger than 250 mm in
diameter, screwdriver, set of turning tools to include
a large gouge and a round-nosed scraper, tailstock
drill chuck to fit your lathe, full-face respirator or
dust mask and goggles, ear defenders, 50 mm
forstner bit, sanding block

OTHER USEFUL TOOLS
cordless screwdriver, power sander, dividers

Turned fruit bowl

250 mm

25 mm

115 mm

40 mm

155 mm

While American oak is used here, you could substitute two different-coloured woods to achieve a counterbalanced colour effect, for added interest.

Materials

American oak (see cutting list)

PVA glue

countersunk steel screws to fit lathe face plate

sandpaper grades 100 to 300

vegetable oil

lint-free cotton cloth to apply the vegetable oil

Cutting List

all pieces cut from American oak

1 piece 250 x 250 x 40 mm (base slab)

3 pieces 250 x 250 x 25 mm (top slabs)

FIG 1

1 Take your planed wood and use the compasses, set at a radius of 125 mm, to set out the four 250 mm-diameter discs. Cut out the discs on the scroll saw (see Fig 1).

FIG 2

2 Smear a generous amount of PVA glue on mating faces, set the wood together in a stack, with all the edges more or less aligned, and clamp up (see Fig 2). Don't worry about the dribbles of glue. Leave for at least 24 hours and then remove the clamps.

FIG 3

3 Set the lathe face plate directly over the centre point of the wood and fix with three or more steel screws (see Fig 3). It is important that the wood is centred and the whole thing is secure. Do not use soft brass or aluminium screws instead of steel, and do not be tempted to curtail the drying time for the glue in step 2.

FIG 4

4 Mount the whole thing on the lathe and set the tool rest just below the centre of spin (see Fig 4). Turn the wood over by hand to make sure that the tool rest is clear.

TIP

Woodturning is potentially dangerous. Put on protective gear and ensure that clothing does not present a hazard.

FIG 5

5 First, use the large gouge to turn the wood to a smooth cylinder 250 mm in diameter, and then turn the cylinder to the shape of the outside of the bowl (see Fig 5). Keep resetting the rest so that it is near the workpiece.

FIG 6

6 Remove the tool rest and fit the 50 mm forstner bit in the tailstock chuck. Slowly advance the tailstock to bore a pilot hole to a depth of about 90 mm, so that it stops about 25 mm short of the bowl bottom (see Fig 6). Keep withdrawing the bit to remove the waste.

FIG 7

7 Move the tool rest so that it is over the bed and very cautiously use the gouge, followed by the scraper, to turn out the centre of the bowl (see Fig 7). Work until you reach the bottom of the drilled pilot hole. When you are pleased with the profile, rub down the bowl with sandpaper and burnish it with vegetable oil.

Kitchen workboards

It is really good to see family and friends using small items that you have made with your own two hands. These simple workboards are a pleasure to make and will be in service for years to come.

Both boards are made from apple wood turned on the lathe. One is decorated by pyrography (branding with a hot iron), while the other is chip carved. Pyrography is very easy: you simply heat the iron and press it into the wood. The chip-carved design is just as straightforward – lots of little boat-shaped knife cuts make a stylized ear of wheat design that is really appropriate for a breadboard. Practise the technique on scrap wood first.

Essential Tools

workbench with vice and holdfast, compass, pencil, rule, scroll saw, lathe with a bowl-turning option and a large face plate, set of turning tools to include a skew chisel, gouge and a round-nosed scraper, full-face respirator or dust mask and goggles, ear defenders, sanding block, dividers, electric soldering iron, small penknife

OTHER USEFUL TOOLS
selection of knives

Kitchen workboards

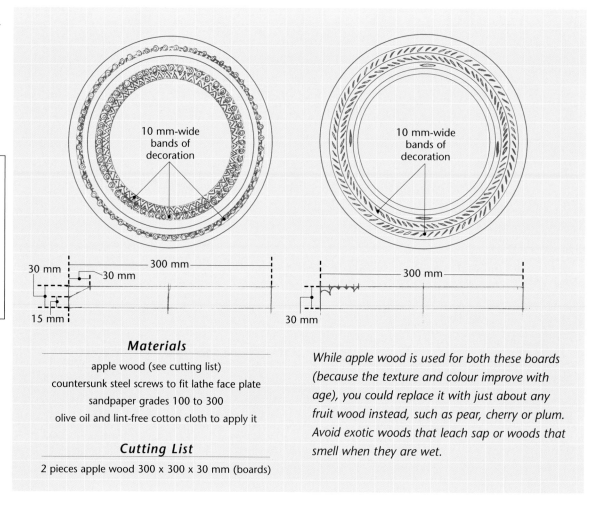

10 mm-wide
bands of
decoration

10 mm-wide
bands of
decoration

30 mm

30 mm

300 mm

15 mm

30 mm

300 mm

Materials

apple wood (see cutting list)

countersunk steel screws to fit lathe face plate

sandpaper grades 100 to 300

olive oil and lint-free cotton cloth to apply it

Cutting List

2 pieces apple wood 300 x 300 x 30 mm (boards)

*While apple wood is used for both these boards
(because the texture and colour improve with
age), you could replace it with just about any
fruit wood instead, such as pear, cherry or plum.
Avoid exotic woods that leach sap or woods that
smell when they are wet.*

PYROGRAPHY BOARD

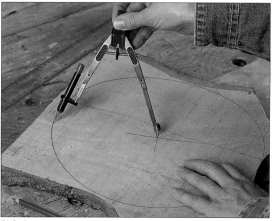

FIG 1

1 Check the slab of wood to make sure that it is absolutely sound throughout, with no knots or splits. Make a point of having a really close look at the end grain, because there is nothing quite so disappointing as going to all the trouble of turning and decorating, only to see the board split in half. Look at the two faces of the board to see which is best. Set your compasses to the largest radius that can be accommodated on the board, and draw a circle on the poorer face (see Fig 1). Mark the centre point with a cross, making sure that it is clearly visible.

FIG 2

2 Prepare the circle for the carved board at the same time as the pyrography board. Fit the scroll saw with a large-toothed blade and adjust the tension so that the blade "pings" when plucked. Fret out the two discs (see Fig 2). These are the blanks for the boards.

TIP

Woodturning is potentially dangerous. Always read the lathe manufacturer's instructions before switching on the power, and work through the following safety checklist.
Always wear a full-face respirator or dust mask and goggles. Remove jewellery and tie back your hair. Never work at a lathe if you are taking medication. Always let someone know before you go off to work on the lathe. Make sure that you are near a phone. If children want to watch, make them wear dust masks, goggles and ear defenders, and keep them well away from the lathe.

FIG 3

FIG 4

3 Set the lathe face plate flat on one of the blanks and align it so that the drawn cross is accurately centred. Clamp the blank to the bench with the holdfast and fix the face plate to the wood with three or more screws (see Fig 3). Mount the face plate securely on the lathe.

4 Adjust the tool rest so that it is just below the centre of spin. Put on your dust mask, goggles and ear defenders. Switch on the power and use the gouge to turn the wood to a smooth disc. Use the skew chisel to turn a slope around the edge (see Fig 4).

FIG 5

FIG 6

5 When you have achieved a crisp disc, take a fold of medium-grade sandpaper and rub the surface to a smooth finish. Set the dividers to 10 mm and use them to scribe a series of step-offs around the border (see Fig 5). Scribe as many step-offs as you want to decorate.

6 Remove the board from the face plate. Switch on the soldering iron and wait until it is red-hot. Have a practice run on some scrap wood to create a design that you like. Burn the design into the board (see Fig 6). Finally, give it a rub-down with olive oil.

CARVED BOARD

FIG 7

FIG 8

7 Mount the sawn blank on the lathe as described in step 3 for the pyrography board. Turn it to a smooth disc, and then with the skew chisel, round over the edge of the disc so that it is nicely convex in cross-section (see Fig 7). Use sandpaper to tidy up the edge and rub the central plateau to a good finish.

8 Continue shaping the edge of the disc until you have a border about 50 mm wide. Set the dividers to 10 mm and run three step-offs around the centre of the border. Take the round-nosed scraper and sculpt a gully on the innermost edge of the border (see Fig 8). Remove the disc from the lathe and sand the back.

FIG 9

9 Put the disc on the bench. With the small penknife, work around the outer border cutting a series of stop-cuts – cuts that run to a depth of about 3 mm. Run a second series of cuts alongside the first to remove boat-shaped chips of wood and create little pockets (see Fig 9).

FIG 10

10 Repeat the chip-cutting procedure as described, only this time work in the opposite direction so that the chips form a chevron, like a stylized ear of wheat (see Fig 10). Brush away the dust and debris, check that the back is smooth, give the wood a wipe over with olive oil, and the board is ready to use.

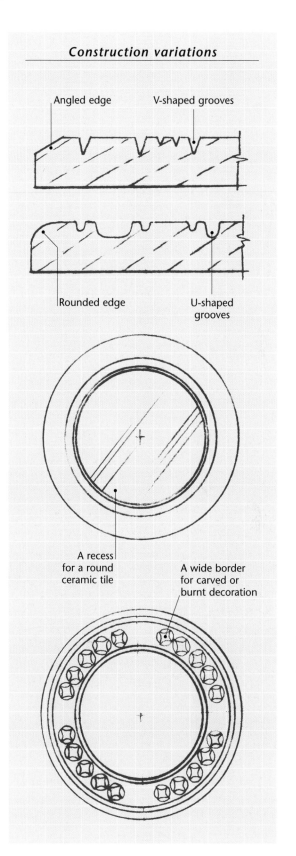

Construction variations

Angled edge   V-shaped grooves

Rounded edge   U-shaped grooves

A recess for a round ceramic tile

A wide border for carved or burnt decoration

TV and video table

This table is the perfect solution if your television is in danger of being obscured by unsteady piles of video tapes and ugly cables and wires. It neatly houses your equipment, hides the wires and, thanks to its triangular shape, fits snugly in the corner of a room.

Apart from a couple of dowels, the table is made from birch plywood throughout, and has four swivel wheels on the underside. The idea is that the television sits on the top surface, the video recorder slides on one shelf, videotapes and magazines are stored on the other, and the cables run out of the back corner of the table directly to the sockets. With the surfaces left natural and wiped over with oil, the table is functional, modern and attractive.

If you like the overall idea of the project, but would prefer to have four shelves, or you want to include a rack for videotapes, the design is flexible enough to allow for modifications and you can adapt it to suit your needs.

─────────── Essential Tools ───────────

workbench with vice and holdfast, pencil,
rule, compasses, square, block plane, sanding
block, jigsaw, electric drill, 12 mm forstner bit,
7 mm counter-bore bit with a plug cutter to match,
screwdriver, awl, paintbrush

OTHER USEFUL TOOLS
cordless screwdriver, power sander, marking knife

TV and video table

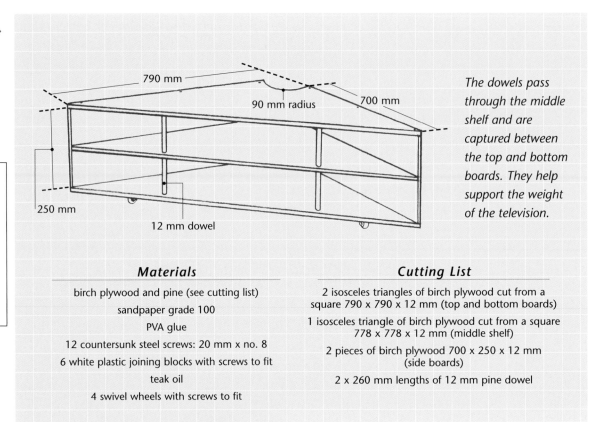

790 mm

90 mm radius

700 mm

250 mm

12 mm dowel

The dowels pass through the middle shelf and are captured between the top and bottom boards. They help support the weight of the television.

You'll need to know

CUTTING CURVED SHAPES
p.16

SCREWING
p.22

NATURAL FINISHES
p.24

Materials

birch plywood and pine (see cutting list)

sandpaper grade 100

PVA glue

12 countersunk steel screws: 20 mm x no. 8

6 white plastic joining blocks with screws to fit

teak oil

4 swivel wheels with screws to fit

Cutting List

2 isosceles triangles of birch plywood cut from a square 790 x 790 x 12 mm (top and bottom boards)

1 isosceles triangle of birch plywood cut from a square 778 x 778 x 12 mm (middle shelf)

2 pieces of birch plywood 700 x 250 x 12 mm (side boards)

2 x 260 mm lengths of 12 mm pine dowel

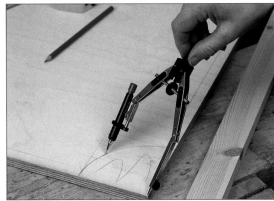

FIG 1

1 Take the top and bottom boards, and the middle shelf, and clean up the edges with the block plane and sandpaper. Make sure that the top and bottom boards are absolutely identical in size. With the pencil, rule a 12 mm border on the face of the top and bottom boards,

on what will be the side edges (this indicates where the edge of the side board underneath is). Set the compasses to 90 mm, spike on the right-angled corner of the triangle and strike off a quarter-circle (see Fig 1). Do this on all three boards.

FIG 2

2 Use the holdfast to secure the workpiece to the bench – so that the right-angled corner is well clear – and then take the jigsaw and fret out the corner detail (see Fig 2). Repeat this procedure on all three boards.

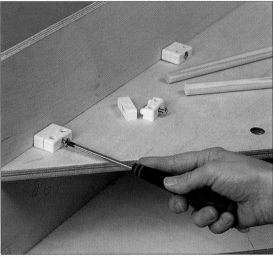

FIG 3

3 Drill the dowel holes with the 12 mm bit. The holes go right through the middle shelf and only half-way through the inside face of the top and bottom boards. Drill holes for the screws with the 7 mm counter-bore bit. Glue and screw the top board to the side boards. Cut plugs and glue them over the screwheads. Fix the middle shelf with the plastic joining blocks (see Fig 3).

FIG 4

4 Slide the two 12 mm dowels into place, and drill, glue and screw the bottom board into position (see Fig 4). Plug the screws as for the top board. Rub down everything with the graded sandpapers and apply some teak oil.

FIG 5

5 Turn the table over so that the underside of the bottom board is uppermost and draw in the position of the four swivel wheels. Make holes with the awl and screw the wheels in place (see Fig 5). Finally, give the top surface another rub-down with the finest grade of sandpaper, followed by another coat of teak oil. Oil the whole table several more times over the next 48 hours.

TIP

If you like the idea of the project but want to cut costs and go for a more basic structure, you could use faced particleboard instead of plywood, and miss out the glue and screws and use the plastic fixing blocks throughout.

Studio table

Designed to complement the Adjustable porch chair on page 128, this table is an absolute classic – a truly beautiful piece of high-quality modern furniture, a piece that draws its inspiration from medieval trestle tables.

Made from American oak throughout, it looks equally at home in the studio or dining room. The secret of its appeal is the choice of wood, the generous width and thickness of the boards, and the simplicity of the design. The great thing about the table is that it can be made without cutting any joints: the boards are simply butted or sandwiched and then fitted with hex-head bolts that run through the thickness of the wood. The two X-frames that make up the legs are linked by the tabletop and the under-stretchers in such a way that the whole structure becomes stable. To finish the surface, the wood is wire-brushed to give it a weathered texture and then wiped with Danish oil. If you like this design but are put off by the price of American oak, the alternative is not to reduce costs by buying thinner boards, but to opt for pine instead and slightly increase the thickness of the boards you purchase.

Essential Tools

workbench with vice, compasses, pencil, rule, square, bevel gauge, clamps, bench drill press, 10 mm forstner bit, 5 mm twist bit, crosscut saw, block plane, wire brush, sanding block, paintbrush, pilot-countersink bit, electric drill, a screwdriver bit, hacksaw, metal file, allen key to fit the hex-heads, screwdriver

OTHER USEFUL TOOLS
power sander

Studio table

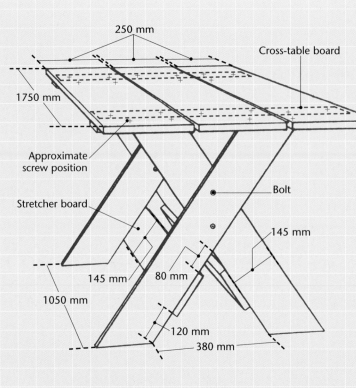

250 mm

Cross-table board

1750 mm

Approximate
screw position

Stretcher board

Bolt

145 mm

145 mm   80 mm

1050 mm

120 mm

380 mm

*The dimensions of this table and the position of the legs
make it suitable for seating six people – one at each end
and two on each side.*

You'll need to know

DRILLING HOLES
p.17

SPECIAL FINISHES
p.25

SCREWING
p.22

Materials

American oak (see cutting list)

sandpaper grades 100 to 300

Danish oil

20 countersunk steel screws:
35 mm x no. 8

4 bolts: steel and
brass hex-head fasteners
complete with threaded
steel rod to fit

8 countersunk steel screws:
75 mm x no. 8

Cutting List

all pieces cut from American oak

4 pieces 920 x 145 x 22 mm
(leg boards)

3 pieces 1750 x 250 x 22 mm
(tabletop boards)

2 pieces 755 x 145 x 22 mm
(cross-table boards)

2 pieces 1050 x 145 x 22 mm
(stretcher boards)

2 pieces 145 x 25 x 22 mm
(distance blocks)

FIG 1

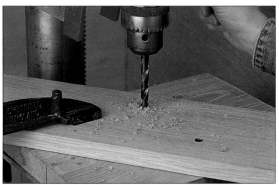

FIG 2

1 Take the four 920 mm leg boards, measure
100 mm along from each end, and use the
bevel gauge to run a line across from the
100 mm mark to the corner (see Fig 1).

2 Set the leg boards together to form the X-
frames and clamp. Mark in the various
screw and bolt holes. Drill the holes – 5 mm
for the screws and 10 mm for the bolts (see Fig 2).

FIG 3

3 Use the crosscut saw to cut the leg boards to shape. Plane the end grain to a good finish. Use the wire brush to scour out the soft part of the grain, so that the surface feels furrowed to the touch (see Fig 3). Sand lightly. Give all the boards a couple of coats of Danish oil.

FIG 4

4 Set the three 250 mm-wide tabletop boards face down on the workbench with 15 mm-thick spacers of scrap wood to keep them apart. Place the two cross-table boards in position, and check with the square to make sure the angle between the legs and the table surface is 90°. Drill holes with the pilot-countersink bit and screw them in place using the screwdriver attachment on the drill. Use two 35 mm screws for each crossover of the two boards (see Fig 4). The two cross-table boards should be 1072 mm apart.

FIG 5

5 Cut the threaded rod to length with the hacksaw (to suit the brass hex-heads) and file the ends so that they run smoothly into the hex-heads. Slide the rods through the X-frame leg boards, thread on the hex-heads, and clench them with the allen key (see Fig 5).

FIG 6

6 Butt the X-frame leg boards against the cross-table board, fit and clamp one of the distance blocks and fix with 75 mm screws (see Fig 6). Do this at both ends of the table. Finally, set the stretcher boards in place, on what will be the underside of the X-frame legs, and screw them in position with 35 mm screws.

Turned table lamp

This contemporary lamp can be used in any room if you fit an appropriate shade. The shape of the form can also be modified to suit your tastes, and the size and power of your lathe.

The lamp base is made from pine throughout. Four small square sections are each planed along one arris (sharp edge) and then glued together in such a way that the four cut-away corners form the flex hole. While the form is still on the lathe, it is stained with a felt-tip pen and burnished with wax. This is a nice, straightforward project if you are new to woodturning – it's inexpensive and there is no need to drill a deep hole for the lamp flex. Although a pen is used here to stain the wood, you could also use a spirit-based wood dye, or even a water-based wood dye followed by a coat of varnish. This lamp is made from four sections; however if anyone offers you a single chunk of seasoned pine, don't turn it down.

Essential Tools

workbench with vice, compasses, pencil, rule, smoothing plane, 4 short sash clamps, bench drill press, 50 mm forstner bit, good-size lathe with an expanding chuck and the capacity to turn a blank bigger than 250 mm in diameter, set of turning tools to include a large gouge, a skew chisel and a round-nosed scraper, full-face respirator or dust mask and goggles, ear defenders, screwdriver

OTHER USEFUL TOOLS
cordless screwdriver, power sander

Turned table lamp

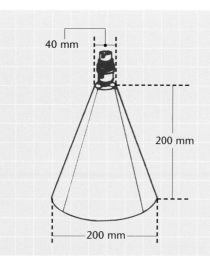

40 mm

200 mm

200 mm

**You'll need
to know**

**HAND PLANING
p.18**

**WOODTURNING
p.23**

**NATURAL FINISHES
p.24**

Make sure that the four pine sections you buy are properly seasoned, otherwise the turned form will shrink and split.

Materials

pine (see cutting list)

PVA glue

sandpaper grades 100 to 150

a couple of spirit-based black felt-tip markers

beeswax polish

lint-free cotton cloth to apply the beeswax

lamp head complete with flex,
plug and screws to fit

lampshade to suit

Cutting List

4 pieces pine 200 x 100 x 100 mm

TIP

Woodturning is potentially dangerous, so be very aware of safety. Always make sure you are suitably dressed, with no dangling hair or jewellery, and no flapping cuffs. Always wear a dust mask and goggles, or a full-face respirator mask; ear defenders are also recommended. Keep children away.

FIG 1

1 Take the four 200 mm-long pine sections and group them four-square so that the best faces are outermost. Plane back the central corners 10 mm (see Fig 1).

FIG 2

2 Regroup the blocks, clamping them together in a trial run to ensure that the mating faces come together tight and true. If necessary, use the plane to cut back the faces. Take the stack apart. Then smear PVA glue on the mating faces of two neighbouring blocks and clamp up (see Fig 2). Repeat this procedure with the other two blocks. When the glue is dry, glue and clamp the paired blocks to make the single four-block blank with a small central hole.

FIG 3

3 Tap a stick of scrap in each end of the central hole. Use the 50 mm forstner bit to bore to a depth of about 10 mm in one end of the block. Mount the blank on the expanding chuck and draw up the tailstock centre (see Fig 3). Turn the wood over by hand to test all is correct.

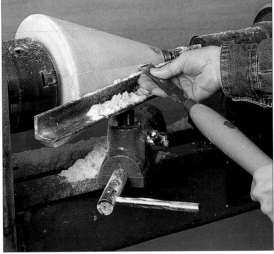

FIG 5

5 Use the gouge to turn the cylinder into a rough cone shape (the base of the cone is nearest to the expanding chuck). Change over to the round-nosed scraper and skew chisel and continue turning until the lines of the cone are clean and smooth (see Fig 5).

FIG 4

4 Arrange the tool rest so that it is clear of the workpiece. Put on the protective gear and tie back your hair. Use the large gouge to turn the square section into the largest possible cylinder (see Fig 4). Use the skew chisel to skim the wood to a smooth finish. Tighten up the tailstock centre.

FIG 6

6 Take the felt-tip pen and run it up and down the spinning cone until the surface is completely black (see Fig 6). Do this several times to ensure even coverage. Use the sandpaper and beeswax to burnish the surface to a high-shine finish. Screw-fit the lamp head to the top of the cone, join up the flex and attach the shade.

Bathroom cabinet

This attractive little cabinet is mainly made from pine and it comes complete with a rail, two doors, a carved turnbuckle, two whittled knobs and routed details. The two shelves are housed in the end boards, while the three vertical posts are dowelled into the shelves, and the rail is captured between the end boards. To finish, it is rubbed down with graded sandpapers and wiped with teak oil.

Essential Tools

workbench with vice and holdfast, compass, pencil,
rule, square, tracing paper, scroll saw, router and
router table, 4 mm and 13 mm groove cutters,
cove cutter, 2 long sash clamps, bench drill press,
15 mm forstner bit, electric drill, 6 mm twist bit,
6 mm dowel marker studs, mallet, penknife,
screwdriver, sanding block, paintbrush

OTHER USEFUL TOOLS
cordless screwdriver, power sander, dividers,
marking knife

Bathroom cabinet

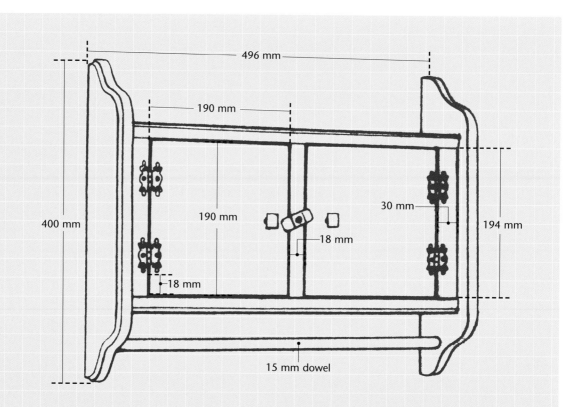

496 mm

190 mm

400 mm

190 mm

30 mm

194 mm

18 mm

18 mm

15 mm dowel

**You'll need
to know**

**CUTTING CURVED
SHAPES**
p.16

**ROUTING EDGE
PROFILES**
p.21

WHITTLING
p.23

Materials

pine and plywood (see cutting list)

guide strip of waste wood: 350 mm long

12 x 30 mm fixing dowels, 6 mm in diameter

PVA glue

1 brass dome-headed screw: 30 mm x no. 8

sandpaper grades 100 to 150

4 decorative brass hinges with brass screws to
fit: size and design to suit

teak oil

Cutting List

2 pieces pine 400 x 150 x 18 mm (end boards)

2 pieces pine 476 x 126 x 18 mm (shelf boards)

1 piece plywood 476 x 210 x 4 mm (back board)

3 pieces pine 194 x 30 x 18 mm (vertical battens)

476 mm length of 15 mm pine dowel (rail)

2 pieces pine 190 x 190 x 18 mm (doors)

*The length of the vertical battens allows for
slightly loose-fitting doors, to avoid problems if
the wood gets damp and expands. The template
below is for half of an end board.*

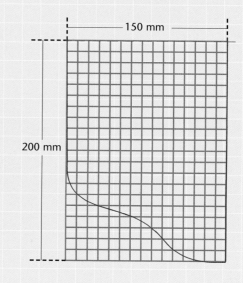

150 mm

200 mm

FIG 1

1 Take the 150 mm-wide end boards and use the pencil, square, rule and tracing paper to carefully set out all the lines that go to make up the design (see Fig 1). Although 150 mm-wide boards at 400 mm long are called for here, it is fine if you can get the design out of boards left over from another project. In this project, a wider piece of wood flawed by a couple of badly placed knots is used.

FIG 2

2 Label the best faces of the two end boards and then fret out the marked design on the scroll saw (see Fig 2). Work slowly, feeding the wood forward so that the blade is presented with the line of next cut. If you feel the blade pulling or the workpiece going off course, ease back and realign the cut. If the going gets heavy, switch off the power and check the blade. Maybe the blade needs changing or re-tensioning, or alternatively, perhaps the wood is damp.

TIP

Routers are potentially dangerous, so you must follow the manufacturer's guidelines carefully. Always keep your fingers well away from the cutter. Wear a full-face respirator and ear defenders while working. At the end of a task, clean up the dust and debris, carefully put the cutters back in the box, and pull out the plug.

FIG 3

3 Fit the 13 mm groove cutter in the router and attach the router to its table. Set one of the end boards flat on the bench, with the inside face uppermost, and clamp it into position. Clamp the guide strip across the board so that the router is able to run alongside it, with the cutter centred on the marked-out housing groove. Plunge the router forward and cut the groove. Make several passes to end up with a depth of 18 mm. Re-run this procedure for all four housings. With the bench drill press and the 15 mm bit, drill the rail holes to a depth of about 8 mm.

When you are ready to cut the cove detail on the shelf ends and edges, fit the cove cutter in the router, and move the fence back out of the way. Switch on the power, wait until the bit is running at full speed, and follow the bearing guide to make the cut (see Fig 3). If you are new to the procedure, have a trial run on some scrap wood.

FIG 4

5 Use the dowel marker studs to transfer the dowel positions from the shelf through to the ends of the vertical battens. The middle batten is pivoted so that it presents the 18 mm thickness. Sink the holes with the 6 mm twist bit to a depth of 25 mm (see Fig 5). Push the fixing dowels in. Use a small wrap of masking tape around the twist bit to act as a depth guide when drilling. Lightly sand the holes with a twist of sandpaper, until the dowels are a good push-fit.

4 Fit the 4 mm groove cutter in the router, slide the fence up to 5 mm and run a groove along the back edge of the side boards and the inner faces of the two shelves. Take the two shelves, establish the position of the three vertical battens (for the doors to hang on and for the middle post) and use the 6 mm twist bit to drill the holes for the fixing dowels. Finally, fit the 13 mm groove cutter in the router, and run a shoulder 12 mm wide and 3 mm deep on the ends of the two shelves and the faces that will be the outside of the cupboard (see Fig 4).

FIG 6

6 Have a trial dry run to make sure that all the component parts come together well. When you are pleased with the results, smear glue in the housing grooves and in the dowel holes, use the mallet to put everything together, and clamp up (see Fig 6).

With the penknife, whittle the turnbuckle from scrap wood and screw it to the middle post. Note the little dowel that runs through the thickness of the central post to act as a stop for the two doors. Adjust the turnbuckle screw so that the buckle is gripped but not crushed.

FIG 5

FIG 7

you would prefer to miss out, you could fit shop-bought handles or knobs. Drill holes for the knobs and glue them in place on the two doors.

Sand the edges of the doors to a good fit and use your chosen hinges to hang them on the doorposts. Rub down all the surfaces to a smooth finish – especially the leading edges of the two side boards, and the edges of the doors. Wipe away the dust and lay on a coat of teak oil. Finally, give the cabinet another sanding with the finest grade of sandpaper, remove the dust and complete the process with a further coat of teak oil.

7 Remove the clamps and sand all the surfaces to a good finish. Make sure that the rail is free to move in its end holes, and the back board is a loose, easy fit. Take a couple of pieces of scrap left over from the end boards, and whittle them into knobs with the penknife (see Fig 7). You can follow the stalk-like design here or cut them to suit yourself – perhaps two little round shapes. If you are new to whittling or it is something that

TIP

If you are in any way worried about a procedure, it's always a good idea to have a trial run on some scrap wood first. Many woodworkers consider that their first effort is a trial run for the real thing.

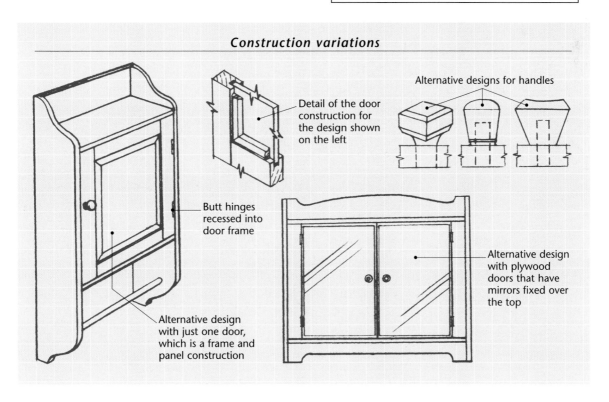

Construction variations

Detail of the door construction for the design shown on the left

Alternative designs for handles

Butt hinges recessed into door frame

Alternative design with just one door, which is a frame and panel construction

Alternative design with plywood doors that have mirrors fixed over the top

Towel rail

While this towel rail has many of the elements that you would expect to see on a classic cottage piece – pierced ends, rounded tops, handle holes, arched foot and an ornate bottom rail – these are no more than stylized interpretations, achieved with the minimum of tools.

The whole thing is made from pine, with the end boards fretted out on the scroll saw, and the bottom rail fretted and then shaped with the spokeshave. All four rails are wedge-tenoned into the end boards. The wood is left in its natural state. It is a very easy item to make – the perfect project for a long weekend. If you like the notion of making a cottage design and yet do not feel up to turning complex rails on a lathe, this project is for you.

Essential Tools

workbench with vice and holdfast, compasses, pencil, rule, square, bench drill press, 12 mm and 55 mm forstner bits, scroll saw, 2 long sash clamps, 12 mm and 20 mm bevel-edge chisels, router and router table, 10 mm groove cutter, spokeshave, sanding block, penknife

OTHER USEFUL TOOLS
cordless screwdriver, power sander, electric drill, dividers, marking knife

Towel rail

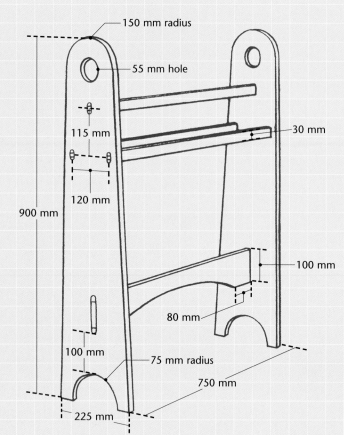

150 mm radius

55 mm hole

115 mm

30 mm

120 mm

900 mm

100 mm

80 mm

100 mm

75 mm radius

750 mm

225 mm

Materials

pine (see cutting list)
sandpaper grades 100 and 120
PVA glue

Cutting List

all pieces cut from pine

2 pieces 900 x 225 x 18 mm
(end boards)

3 pieces 750 x 30 x 18 mm (top rails)

1 piece 750 x 100 x 18 mm
(bottom rail)

This towel rail could also be used as a display stand. Quilts, attractive linens, patchwork and embroidery are good candidates for displaying informally in this manner.

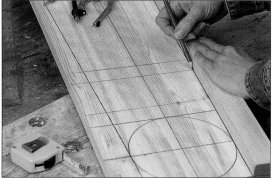

FIG 1

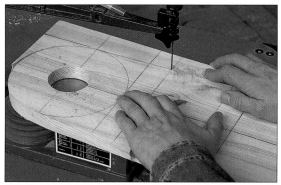

FIG 2

1 Draw in centre-lines on the end boards. Set the compasses to a radius of 75 mm and draw out the top and bottom details. Use the rule to link up the details (see Fig 1).

2 Bore the handle hole with the 55 mm forstner bit and fret out the form on the scroll saw. Cut in from both ends of the wood to meet at the middle (see Fig 2).

FIG 3

FIG 5

3 Drill the ends of the mortise holes with the 12 mm forstner bit. Clamp the workpiece flat on the bench and chop out the remaining waste with the 12 mm bevel-edge chisel (see Fig 3). Work from both sides so that the wood is not damaged when the chisel exits.

5 Cut out the shape of the bottom rail on the scroll saw and then use the spokeshave to bring the sawn edge to a rounded, smoothly curved finish (see Fig 5). Use the spokeshave to chamfer the edges of the three top rails. Sand all the edges and faces to a smooth finish.

FIG 4

FIG 6

4 Fit the 10 mm groove cutter in the router and attach the router to its table. Draw the fence back, and set the bit to a height of 3 mm. Pass the rails through the router and cut shoulders on both side faces. Reduce the bit height to 1.5 mm and cut shoulders on the top and bottom edge faces (see Fig 4).

6 With the penknife and chisels, carefully shape the square ends of the rails to fit the round-ended mortises (see Fig 6). When you have achieved a push-fit, run two saw kerfs (cuts) into the ends of the tenons. Finally, glue and wedge the rails in place, and sand the towel rail to a smooth finish, especially the top of the rails.

Sauna bench

This stylish seat is suitable for a bathroom or sauna, because it resists steam and hot water. Glue is used in its construction. It is designed so that it can be built in the space of a day with the minimum of tools and expertise – there are no joints to make and there is no need for expensive tools. Material costs are low – pine is used instead of expensive endangered species such as mahogany, and the bench is put together without pricey brass or stainless-steel fittings.

This novel design is wonderfully simple – all the components are made from pine section, and the bench is held together with four threaded rods complete with nuts, washers and screws. Costs are kept down by using zinc-plated rod; however you could improve on the quality of the finish by using stainless steel. Note how the inclusion of two stretcher pieces set into the top of the seat acts as an anti-wracking device (stops it twisting) and keeps the structure square.

Essential Tools

workbench with vice and holdfast, pencil, rule, square, bench drill press, 6 mm twist bit, block plane, sanding block, clamps, screwdriver, pair of wrenches to fit the nuts, hacksaw, file

OTHER USEFUL TOOLS
cordless screwdriver, power sander

Sauna bench

You'll need to know

DRILLING HOLES
p.17

HAND PLANING
p.18

SCREWING
p.22

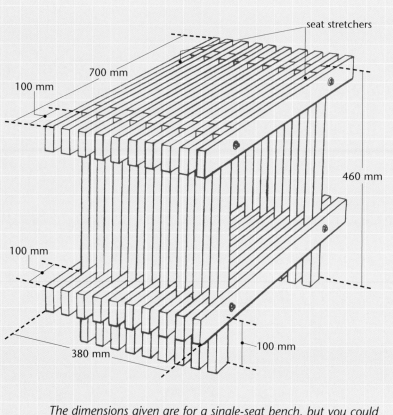

seat stretchers

700 mm

100 mm

460 mm

100 mm

380 mm

100 mm

Materials

pine (see cutting list)

sandpaper grades 100 and 120

4 countersunk steel screws: 30 mm x no. 8

4 x 400 mm lengths of plated 6 mm threaded rod with 8 nuts and 8 washers to fit

Cutting List

all pieces cut from pine

20 pieces 700 x 50 x 20 mm (seat and undershelf)

18 pieces 460 x 50 x 20 mm (legs)

2 pieces 400 x 50 x 20 mm (seat stretchers)

The dimensions given are for a single-seat bench, but you could double the length of the seat and undershelf pieces so that the bench is long enough to stretch out on.

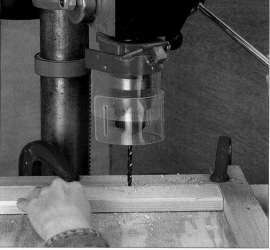

FIG 1

TIP

The jig ensures that holes can be drilled accurately. Run the drill in and out repeatedly, in order to clear the waste from the hole, and to allow the bit to cool down. Brush the debris off the jig after each boring.

1 Mark the position of the holes for the threaded rod – see the working drawing – and build a jig from scrap wood. Clamp the jig to the table of the bench drill press and use the 6 mm bit to bore the holes (see Fig 1).

FIG 2

2 Use the block plane and the medium-grade sandpaper to remove the sharp edges from all 40 component parts (see Fig 2).

FIG 3

3 Clamp and screw the first seat stretcher in place and start sliding the components on to the threaded rods (see Fig 3). Be careful not to damage the thread or split the wood.

FIG 4

4 Ease each piece down the threaded rods, making sure the best edges form the upper surface of the seat (see Fig 4).

FIG 5

5 When you have screwed the other stretcher in place, and fitted the last two seat and undershelf pieces, use the square to ensure that the whole structure is true. Finally, clench the nuts with the wrenches (see Fig 5), saw the ends off the threaded rods with the hacksaw and file them to a smooth finish.

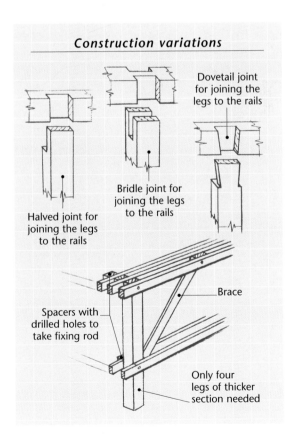

Construction variations

Halved joint for joining the legs to the rails

Bridle joint for joining the legs to the rails

Dovetail joint for joining the legs to the rails

Spacers with drilled holes to take fixing rod

Brace

Only four legs of thicker section needed

Garden trug

This pretty garden trug or basket is reminiscent of the beautiful split wood baskets that were popular in Edwardian times. Prints of the period depicting garden scenes often show the lady of the house gliding around the garden with a parasol in one hand and a trug in the other. A trug is perfectly suited to carrying small tools and garden produce. You might use it when weeding a border, or when cutting flowers. Trugs are also suitable for indoor use – their design makes them ideal as a feature in the kitchen, perhaps for holding cutlery or bread, or even for decorative use as a table centrepiece.

The trug is made from pine throughout. The two side boards are worked on the scroll saw, the slats are pinned in place, the fretted uprights are screwed to the side boards, and the handle is simply captured between the supports. A unique feature of this design is the whittled stretcher handle, which has a curvaceous form and dappled texture. To finish, it is colourwashed with acrylic paint, followed by a couple of coats of teak oil.

Essential Tools

workbench with vice and holdfast, pencil, rule,
compasses, square, bevel gauge, clamp, jigsaw, bench
drill press, 15 mm forstner bit, scroll saw,
pin hammer, screwdriver, knife, block plane,
sanding block, 2 paintbrushes

OTHER USEFUL TOOLS
cordless screwdriver, power sander, electric drill,
marking knife, bandsaw

Garden trug

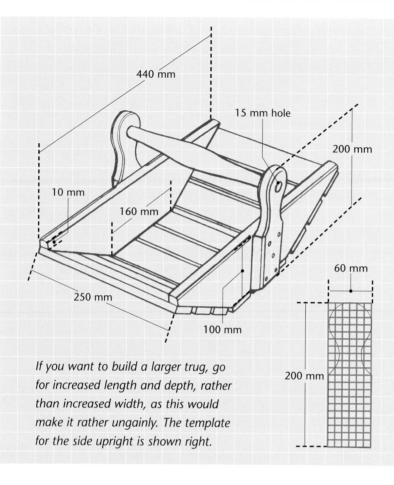

440 mm

15 mm hole

200 mm

10 mm

160 mm

250 mm

100 mm

60 mm

200 mm

If you want to build a larger trug, go for increased length and depth, rather than increased width, as this would make it rather ungainly. The template for the side upright is shown right.

Materials

pine (see cutting list)

36 steel pins: 20 mm

10 countersunk stainless-steel screws: 30 mm x no. 8

sandpaper grades 80 and 100

acrylic paint: colour to suit

teak oil

Cutting List

all pieces cut from pine

2 pieces 440 x 100 x 18 mm (side boards)

9 pieces 250 x 45 x 12 mm (slats)

2 pieces 200 x 60 x 18 mm (side uprights)

1 piece 300 x 40 x 40 mm (stretcher handle)

FIG 1

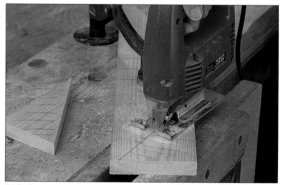

FIG 2

1 Take the two prepared boards at 440 mm long and 100 mm wide, and use the bevel gauge, rule and square to carefully draw out the profile of the sides, complete with the centre-line and the position of the slats (see Fig 1).

2 Clamp the workpiece firmly on the bench so that the waste is hanging clear, and use the jigsaw to cut out the profile to the waste side of the drawn line (see Fig 2). Always cut from the base edge through to the top corner.

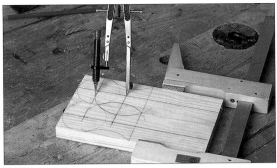

FIG 3

3 Clamp the two 60 mm-wide side uprights together. Use the square, rule and compasses to set out the round-topped shape (see working drawing) complete with a centre-line and the position of the handle hole (see Fig 3).

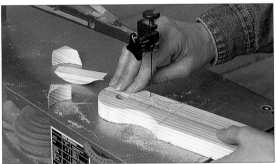

FIG 4

4 Drill the handle holes with the 15 mm forstner bit. Use the scroll saw to fret out the design, with the line of cut set slightly to the waste side of the drawn line (see Fig 4).

FIG 5

5 With the two side boards bottom edge uppermost and parallel to each other, bridge them with the slats. Check the alignment with the square, and then nail the slats in position with two pins at each end (see Fig 5).

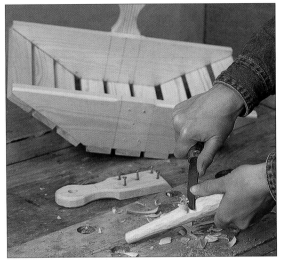

FIG 6

TIP

When you are whittling, control the knife by working with the wood braced tightly against your thumb, and making a "pushing" cut. Keep both the knife and the workpiece moving so you achieve a uniform section. Use a selection of knives of different weights and sizes, to achieve a variety of cuts.

6 Screw one side upright in place. To make the stretcher handle, whittle the 40 mm section to a cylinder with the knife, working from centre to end. Continue until the ends fit the 15 mm holes and the form is nicely curved (see Fig 6). Capture the handle between the two side uprights and fix with screws. Finally, tidy up all the end-grain surfaces with the block plane and rub down the trug with sandpaper. Dilute the paint in water to make a wash and brush on. When it is dry, lay on two coats of teak oil.

Doll's house

Most children really enjoy playing with doll's houses, but many parents find them something of a nuisance. The problem is that they are usually bulky, fragile, and difficult to store. This doll's house can be flat-packed, however. When the children have finished playing with it, you simply pull it apart and slide it under the bed. The design is so simple that you can even let the children put it together themselves, like a construction kit. The design is stylized so that children can let their imaginations run riot: it can be a townhouse, or a cottage, or perhaps a garage for cars, or even a school. There are many exciting possibilities.

The house is made of 6 mm birch plywood, and the various forms are slotted and shaped so that the parts slide together easily. The scroll saw makes it simple to construct. Most of the corners are rounded, and the whole thing is finished with child-friendly acrylic paint. Check with the manufacturer to ensure that a paint really is suitable for applying to a children's toy – it must have no harmful effects if the toy is put in the mouth.

Essential Tools

workbench with vice and holdfast, compasses, pencil,
rule, square, bevel gauge, scroll saw, electric drill,
5 mm and 8 mm twist bits, sanding block,
2 paintbrushes

OTHER USEFUL TOOLS
power sander

Doll's house

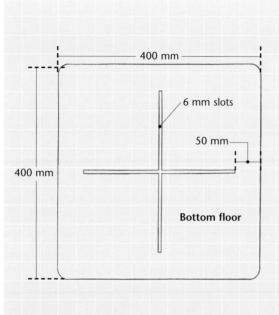

400 mm

6 mm slots

50 mm

400 mm

Bottom floor

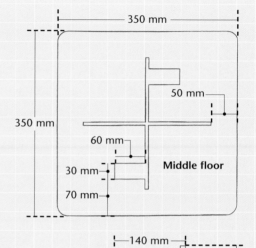

350 mm

350 mm

50 mm

60 mm

30 mm

70 mm

Middle floor

140 mm

8 mm hole

130 mm

60 mm

Stairs

40 mm — 22 mm

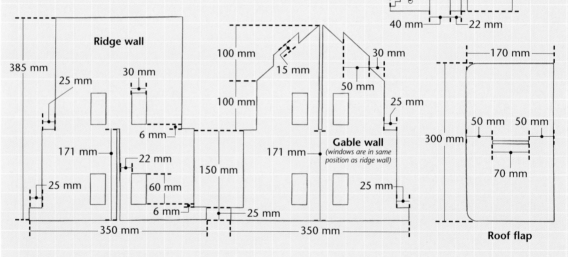

Ridge wall

385 mm

25 mm

30 mm

6 mm

171 mm

22 mm

25 mm

60 mm

6 mm

350 mm

100 mm

15 mm

100 mm

150 mm

25 mm

30 mm

50 mm

25 mm

171 mm

Gable wall
(windows are in same position as ridge wall)

25 mm

350 mm

170 mm

50 mm   50 mm

300 mm

70 mm

Roof flap

The doll's house is suitable for very young children to play with, as there are no tight holes where tiny fingers might get trapped.

Materials

birch plywood and pine (see cutting list)

sandpaper grades 100 and 150

acrylic paint: red, yellow, pink, blue and green

matt acrylic varnish

Cutting List

1 piece birch plywood 400 x 400 x 6 mm
(bottom floor)

1 piece birch plywood 350 x 350 x 6 mm
(middle floor)

2 pieces birch plywood 300 x 170 x 6 mm (roof flaps)

1 piece birch plywood 400 x 350 x 6 mm (ridge wall)

1 piece birch plywood 400 x 350 x 6 mm (gable wall)

4 pieces birch plywood 140 x 130 x 6 mm (stairs)

2 x 40 mm lengths of 8 mm pine dowel

FIG 1

1 Study the working drawings carefully to see how the whole thing works and slots together, and then use the rule, bevel gauge and square to set out each piece of plywood with all the lines that make up the design (see Fig 1). Shade in the waste areas up to the drawn line.

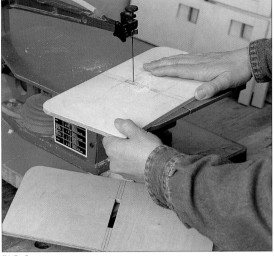

FIG 3

3 When you come to an enclosed area – such as the doors or the roof slots – drill pilot holes with the 5 mm bit. Unhitch the scroll saw blade, pass it through the hole, and then refit it and continue as already described (see Fig 3). Be careful not to twist the blade at the turns.

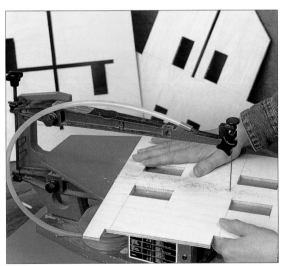

FIG 2

2 Fit a new fine blade in the scroll saw and tension it until it "pings" when plucked, then start fretting out the various parts (see Fig 2). When you are cutting the slots, make sure that you keep on the waste side of the drawn lines, so the slots are exactly 6 mm wide (or to a maximum of 0.5 mm wider, making 6.5 mm).

FIG 4

4 Run through a trial fitting of the two walls (see Fig 4). If the slots are too tight, wrap a sheet of fine-grade sandpaper around a piece of waste plywood and sand them to fit. Aim to increase the width of the slots to a maximum of 6.5 mm. Be careful not to rub so hard that you reveal the inner veneers of the plywood.

FIG 5

5 Slide the bottom floor over the walls and check that it fits well – it should sit flat on all four of the lower support steps. Slide the middle floor in place so that it settles on all four of the upper support steps (see Fig 5). Once again, you might need to adjust the slots with fine-grade sandpaper. The best way of sanding is to rest the workpiece flat on the bench, so that the offending edge is as near as possible to the worksurface.

FIG 6

6 Take one of the stair pieces and draw on a 10 mm grid, the outline of the stairs, arched door and dowel holes. Stack the four stair pieces with the gridded piece uppermost, then drill holes with the 8 mm bit and slide in the dowels. With the scroll saw, cut the shapes of the stairs and door through the whole stack (see Fig 6).

FIG 7

7 Take the sanding block and sandpaper and rub all the edges to a good, smooth finish (see Fig 7). Aim for slightly rounded edges. A good way of testing for burrs or sharp edges that you have missed is to feel the forms with your fingertips, keeping your eyes closed.

TIP

Of all the projects in this book, this is the only one where you cannot cut costs – children's toys must be safe. You must use best-quality birch plywood, because it is strong and splinter-proof. It is essential to use paints (and varnishes) that are described by the manufacturer as being safe for children: on no account use household or car paints, because they may contain toxic substances.

FIG 8

FIG 9

8 Mix the paint with a small amount of water to make a thin wash, apply with a brush (see Fig 8) and then let it dry. If you want the colour to be darker, simply paint on repeat washes until you have the right density of colour. Let the washes dry between coats.

9 When the paint is completely dry – and this might take a couple of days – give the house another rub-down with the graded sandpaper and brush on the varnish. Repeat this procedure a couple of times until the finish feels super-smooth to the touch (see Fig 9).

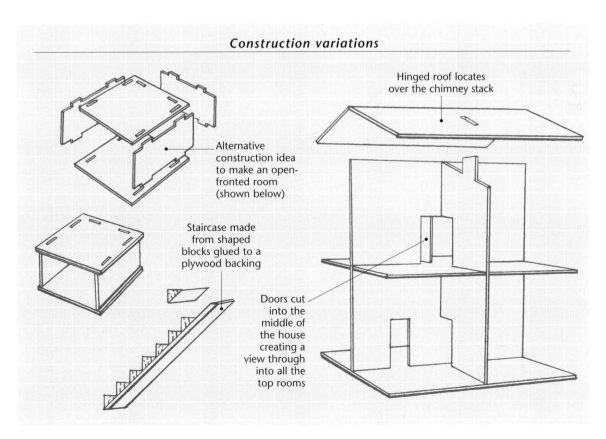

Construction variations

Hinged roof locates over the chimney stack

Alternative construction idea to make an open-fronted room (shown below)

Staircase made from shaped blocks glued to a plywood backing

Doors cut into the middle of the house creating a view through into all the top rooms

Child's folk art chest

This charming chest is made from pine throughout. The front and back boards are screwed to the end boards, with the base board captured and screwed between. Rope handles are threaded and knotted through blocks. The lid is simply set flush with the back and hinged. The painted design is in the style of the naïve designs on old American folk art chests. Although red, white and blue, and stars and stripes, are used here, the chest is not painted with the specific imagery of the American or British flag. The stripes are painted with the aid of masking tape; the stars are created by cutting a star from a scrap of plywood and using it as a stamp.

───────── Essential Tools ─────────

workbench with vice, compasses, pencil, rule, square, scroll saw, electric drill, 6 mm counter-bore bit with a plug cutter to match, screwdriver bit, block plane, clamps, bench drill press, 10 mm and 5 mm twist bits, pilot-countersink bit, sanding block, scissors, 20 mm bevel-edge chisel, artist's paintbrush, screwdriver, paintbrush

OTHER USEFUL TOOLS
power sander

Child's folk art chest

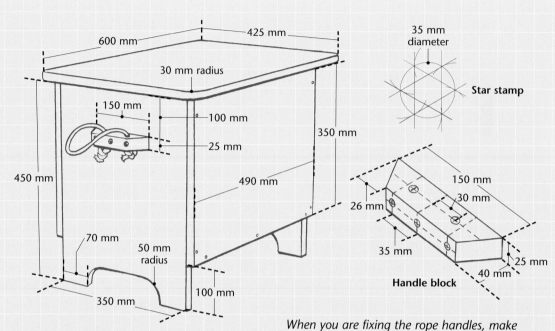

600 mm · 425 mm

35 mm diameter

30 mm radius

Star stamp

150 mm

100 mm

350 mm

25 mm

450 mm

490 mm

150 mm

30 mm

26 mm

70 mm

50 mm radius

35 mm

25 mm

40 mm

Handle block

350 mm

100 mm

You'll need to know

CUTTING CURVED SHAPES
p.16

PAINTED FINISHES
p.25

FIXING HINGES
p.23

When you are fixing the rope handles, make sure that you make the loops much smaller than the size of your child's head, or the handles will present a safety hazard.

Materials

pine (see cutting list)
30 countersunk steel screws: 30 mm x no. 8
PVA glue
sandpaper grades 100 and 150
6 countersunk steel screws: 35 mm x no. 8
2 x 300 mm lengths of soft hemp rope
masking tape and scissors
acrylic paint: red, white and blue
2 steel hinges: 50 x 18 mm with screws to fit
Danish oil

Cutting List

all pieces cut from pine
2 pieces 490 x 350 x 18 mm (front and back boards)
2 pieces 450 x 350 x 18 mm (end boards)
1 piece 454 x 350 x 18 mm (base board)
1 piece 600 x 425 x 18 mm (lid board)
2 pieces 150 x 40 x 25 mm (handle blocks)

FIG 1

1 Check all the wood to make sure that it is free from splits. Take the prepared boards and use the rule, square and compasses to draw out all the lines that make up the design. Set out the curve of the lid corners with a 30 mm radius, and the foot detail on the end boards with a radius of 50 mm (see Fig 1). Double-check the measurements and shade in selected areas to avoid confusion when cutting out. Draw the shape of the handle blocks, complete with holes.

FIG 2

2 Fret out the various shapes on the scroll saw. When you are cutting the curves, run the line of cut to the waste side of the drawn line (see Fig 2). Have a trial fitting to see how the box comes together. Pay particular attention to the fit of the base board.

FIG 4

4 Trim the base board to fit between the sides of the chest and fix with 30 mm screws, using the drill and screwdriver attachment, as described in step 3 (see Fig 4). Turn the chest upright to see whether it stands firm. If it rocks, the feet need trimming with the block plane.

FIG 3

3 With the 6 mm counter-bore bit, drill pilot holes through the front and back boards. Using the drill and screwdriver attachment, screw them to the end boards with the 30 mm screws (see Fig 3). The top edges should be flush. Make checks with the square. Cut plugs with the plug cutter and glue them over the screws.

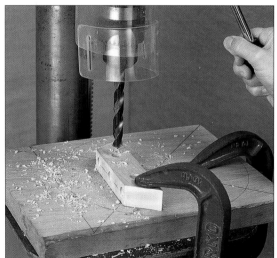

FIG 5

5 Cut the handle blocks with the scroll saw and draw in the position of the holes: two 10 mm holes for the ropes, and three 5 mm holes for the screws. Clamp to the bench drill press and bore the holes (see Fig 5). Countersink the screwholes with the pilot-countersink bit and sand the blocks to a smooth finish.

FIG 6

FIG 8

6 Measure 100 mm down from the top of the chest, and centre and screw the handle blocks in place with 35 mm screws (see Fig 6). Take a 300 mm length of rope, thread it through the holes and knot the ends. Do figure-of-eight knots so they cannot slip and come undone.

8 Position the chest with the front face uppermost. Measure 50 mm in from all four edges and use the pencil and rule to draw a border or frame. Divide up the inside area vertically, so that you have four equal horizontal bands each about 60 mm wide. From top to bottom number the bands 1, 2, 3, and 4. Cover the outer frame and bands 2 and 4 with masking tape. Smooth the tape in place. Brush red acrylic paint over bands 1 and 3, painting well over the edges of the tape. Leave it to dry (see Fig 8).

FIG 7

7 To make the stamp, set the compasses to a radius of 35 mm and draw a circle on scrap wood. With the compasses at the same radius, make step-offs around the circumference of the circle and strike arcs. Use the pencil and rule to draw lines between alternate intersections, so you end up with a six-pointed star (see Fig 7).

FIG 9

9 When the red paint is dry, carefully peel off the horizontal strips of tape to reveal beautiful, crisp edges (see Fig 9). Stick masking tape over the bands of red to safeguard them.

FIG 11

11 Fret out the star on the scroll saw, sand the edges to a smooth finish, and drive a 30 mm screw into its centre to use like a handle. Spread a generous daub of white paint on a piece of card, then press the star in the paint and start stamping (see Fig 11). Try to do the stamping with a crisp on-and-off action, so the images do not smudge.

FIG 10

10 Paint the bands that you have just revealed with blue paint (see Fig 10). Let the paint dry and carefully peel away all the masking tape on the bands and borders. You should be left with a crisply painted panel. At this point, if you so wish, you could paint similar bands on the lid of the chest.

TIP

If you like the idea of a printed design, but are not keen on the stars, you could cut an alternative shape, or try using other items as stamps, such as corks or leaves. Use paint straight from the tube or bottle, so that it is a thick consistency and will not run.

FIG 12

12 Finally, when the paint is dry, use the chisel to cut recesses for the hinges and screw them in place. Give all the surfaces a rub-down with fine-grade sandpaper, followed by a coat of Danish oil (see Fig 12).

Kitchen trolley

Now at last you can have the custom-made kitchen trundle trolley of your dreams! A modern classic, this beautifully designed kitchen workstation is made from cool, blonde maple. The woven basket drawer is English willow, the towel bar is stainless steel, the worktop is made from chunky sections, and the trolley is mounted on four super-smooth swivel-turn wheels. This is an amazingly stylish and functional piece – perfect for the modern home.

As for the making process, study the designs first, purchase a ready-made willow basket, the wheels and stainless-steel fittings, and then modify the dimensions and details to suit your needs. It's an easy project to build. The horizontal members – the front and back stretchers, and the back rail – are tenoned into the legs to make two H-frames, and then the two frames are linked by the side rails, the top board and the shelf slats. The wheels are bolted into pilot holes, while the top slab is held in place with screwed blocks and turnbuckles. The wood is finished by repeatedly rubbing down, oiling, waxing and burnishing to a sheen finish with a cotton cloth.

Essential Tools

workbench with vice, pencil, rule, square, biscuit jointer, 4 sash clamps or clamp heads, good selection of G-clamps, jigsaw, block plane, scraper plane, bench drill press, 25 mm forstner bit, 3 mm and 5 mm twist bits and a twist bit to fit the diameter of your wheel bolts, 15 mm bevel-edge chisel, mallet, mitre saw, router and router table, 12 mm groove cutter, knife, tenon saw, smoothing plane, screwdriver, sanding block, pilot-countersink bit, socket and wrench to fit the size of your wheel bolt, paintbrush

OTHER USEFUL TOOLS
cordless screwdriver, power sander, electric drill, dividers, marking knife, bandsaw

Kitchen trolley

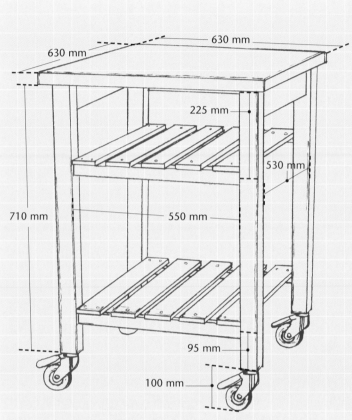

630 mm

630 mm

710 mm

225 mm

530 mm

550 mm

95 mm

100 mm

You'll need to know

HAND CUTTING A MORTISE
p.18

HAND CUTTING A TENON
p.19

ROUTING A MORTISE
p.19

Materials

maple (see cutting list)

pack of jointer biscuits

PVA glue

sandpaper grades 150 to 300

4 swivel-turn wheels (integral foot brakes), to stand about 100 mm from the floor

Danish oil

28 countersunk stainless-steel screws: 30 mm x no. 8

stainless-steel towel rack

Cutting List

all pieces cut from maple

5 pieces 630 x 140 x 30 mm (worktop)

4 pieces 710 x 50 x 50 mm (legs)

2 pieces 530 x 80 x 20 mm (side rails)

1 piece 510 x 80 x 20 mm (back rail)

4 pieces 550 x 30 x 30 mm (stretchers)

10 pieces 590 x 70 x 12 mm (shelf slats)

If your wheels are a different size to those specified, be sure to adjust the length of the legs accordingly.

FIG 1

1 Take the five prepared boards for the worktop (630 mm long, 140 mm wide), and place them side by side so that the end grain in neighbouring planks runs in different directions.

Mark in the position of the biscuit joints at the centre and 50 mm from the ends. Set the biscuit jointer to 15 mm and cut the slots on the five boards. Blow out the dust and spread glue on the mating faces of the biscuits and the boards, and clamp up. Use three sash clamps, plus the G-clamps, to hold the joints in place (see Fig 1).

When the glue is completely dry, remove the clamps and move the slab to a clean, level surface. Finally, use the jigsaw, block plane and scraper plane to work the slab to a smooth, clean-edged finish, 630 mm square. Remove all traces of glue.

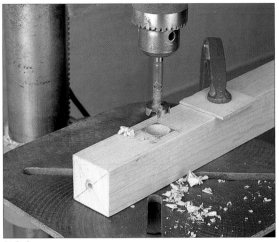

FIG 2

FIG 4

2 Take the four 710 mm legs and mark the top and bottom. Set out mortises 25 mm square, at centres 225 mm down from the top and 95 mm up from the bottom. Draw crossed diagonals to establish the position of the wheel bolts. Drill the mortises with the 25 mm forstner bit, to a depth of 40 mm. Drill holes in the ends of the legs to fit your wheel bolts (see Fig 2).

4 Take the four 550 mm stretchers and set out the tenons by measuring 40 mm from the ends. Set the mitre saw depth gauge to 2.5 mm and saw the tenon shoulders (see Fig 4). Use the chisel to pare the tenons to fit. Aim for a tight push-fit, with the shoulders of the tenon sitting square and flush with the face of the leg. Test it is square with the square.

FIG 3

FIG 5

3 Clamp the legs to the bench and use the bevel-edge chisel and the mallet to work the bored holes into crisp, blind mortises 25 mm square and 40 mm deep (see Fig 3). Scrape the bottom of the mortise to a clean finish and remove all the debris. Be careful not to lever the tool against the side of the mortise.

5 Mark out open rail mortises on the legs, at 75 mm long, 12 mm wide and 20 mm deep, and centred so that the rails are set 10 mm back from the face. Attach the router to its table, fit the 12 mm groove cutter, set the fence to 14 mm, clamp a depth-stop block made from an offcut at 75 mm, and rout the mortises (see Fig 5).

FIG 6

6 Mark the ends of the rails at 20 mm. Rout the stepped tenons, making them 20 mm long, 75 mm wide and 12 mm thick. Use the knife to whittle the stepped underside so that it fits into the 12 mm open mortise (see Fig 6).

FIG 7

7 Plane the worktop to a square finish with the smoothing plane. Use the biscuit jointer to cut grooves on the inside face of both side rails. Use the tenon saw to cut turnbuckles and screw blocks (see Fig 7) from scrap wood to fit.

Clear the workbench of accumulated clutter and use a vacuum cleaner to remove all small pieces of debris. If the top of your workbench is badly scarred or covered in hard blobs of glue, cover it with a sheet of clean plywood to work on. It is vital that the surface is perfectly clean. Set the worktop face down on the workbench or ply-

wood, and have a trial dry-run fitting of the legs, stretchers and rails (see Fig 7).

When you are happy with the way it all comes together, spread glue in the joints and clamp up. When the glue is dry, remove the clamps, screw the blocks and the turnbuckles in place to hold the worktop to the rails, and use the chisel and the sandpaper to remove all traces of dried glue.

TIP

To avoid drill chatter and friction burns when countersinking the holes, fix the drill's depth gauge to 5 mm and then swiftly and firmly run the countersink bit in and out. Make sure the drill is running at full speed before the bit strikes the wood.

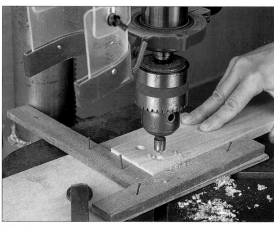

FIG 8

8 Take two of the shelf slats and mark out the position of the screwholes 25 mm from the ends – one with a single hole at the centre and the other with two holes 20 mm in from the sides. Double-check your measurements.

Use the two slats to build a jig from scrap wood, and then drill all the slats with the 5 mm twist bit and the pilot-countersink bit (see Fig 8).

Make sure, after every drilling, that you stop and use a brush to remove the sawdust from the corners of the jig. Work carefully so that the drill bit enters and exits leaving clean holes.

FIG 9

FIG 10

9 Clear all the dust and fragments of wood off the workbench and set the trolley upside-down on the bench, so that the ends of the legs are at a comfortable height. With the socket and wrench, bolt the wheels in place (see Fig 9). Go over the trolley with the block plane, cleaning up ends and skimming off sharp corners. Make sure that all traces of glue have been removed. To this end, take the trolley outside the workshop, so that you can view it in full daylight, and inspect all the areas around the joints. A good test is to brush the surface with white spirit, which will highlight any areas of glue. Finally, sweep up the debris and wipe the dust off with a cotton cloth.

10 Move to a clean area and brush the whole trolley with a thin coat of Danish oil, working over the frame with the worktop in place and the ten loose slats.

Set the two-hole slats to bridge the stretchers, so that they are hard up against the legs with the ends flush (see Fig 10). Drill 3 mm pilot holes and fix the slats in place with the stainless-steel screws. Set out the single-hole slats with a spacing of 30 mm and repeat the screwing procedure. To ensure that the spacing is uniform, cut a strip of waste 30 mm wide, and set it between neighbouring slats before driving the screws home. Screw the stainless-steel rail in place.

Construction variations

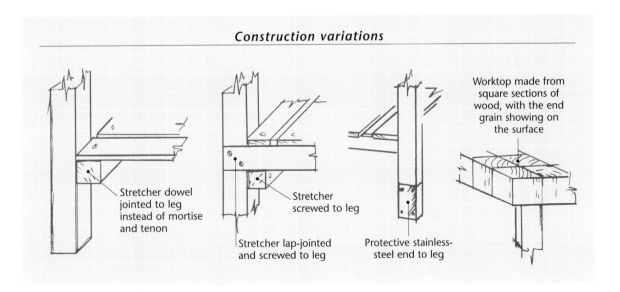

Stretcher dowel jointed to leg instead of mortise and tenon

Stretcher screwed to leg

Stretcher lap-jointed and screwed to leg

Protective stainless-steel end to leg

Worktop made from square sections of wood, with the end grain showing on the surface

French cupboard

This pretty little herb cupboard is lifted above the ordinary by beautifully delicate curves at top and bottom, a colourwashed finish, and a whittled handle that doubles as a catch.

The cupboard is made from good-quality pine tongue-and-groove boards for the front, back, sides and shelves; pine sections for the door battens and shelf supports inside, to hold the whole thing together; and an offcut for the handle. The surface is colourwashed with a mixture of acrylic paint and water, and finally wiped over with teak oil. A mix of blue and green is used here to achieve a greenish tinge, but you can opt for any colour that appeals, such as a strong red, or even a limewashed finish.

Essential Tools

workbench with vice, pencil, rule, square,
smoothing plane, screwdriver, scroll saw, sanding block,
mitre saw, 7 mm counter-bore bit with a plug cutter to
match, knife, electric drill, 10 mm and 3 mm twist bits,
awl, 2 paintbrushes

OTHER USEFUL TOOLS
cordless screwdriver, power sander, marking knife

French cupboard

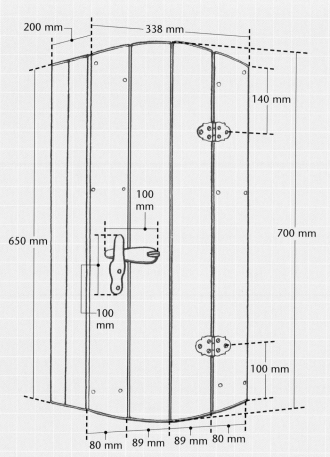

200 mm

338 mm

140 mm

100 mm

700 mm

650 mm

100 mm

100 mm

80 mm 89 mm 89 mm 80 mm

You'll need to know

SCREWING
p.22

CUTTING CURVED SHAPES
p.16

WHITTLING
p.23

Materials

pine (see cutting list)

50+ countersunk steel screws:
35 mm x no. 8

sandpaper grades 80 and 150

2 surface-mounted brass hinges
(design and size to suit) with screws to fit

acrylic paint: colour to suit

teak oil

Cutting List

all pieces cut from pine

4 pieces of tongue-and-groove
700 x 89 x 15 mm (front boards, consisting
of 2 doors and 2 side pieces)

4 pieces of tongue-and-groove
650 x 89 x 15 mm (back boards)

4 pieces of tongue-and-groove
650 x 89 x 15 mm (side boards)

3 pieces 312 x 170 x 18 mm (shelves)

8 pieces 160 x 30 x 18 mm
(2 door battens and 6 shelf supports)

If you want to carve a more complex catch than this one (which is made of leftover scraps), consider using a piece of easy-to-carve lime.

FIG 1

FIG 2

1 Study the design and note how all the boards that meet at the corners have been reduced in width. Now take the smoothing plane and trim the boards to size (see Fig 1).

2 Take the two boards that make the door and screw them together with two 160 mm door battens. Use two staggered screws on each board width (see Fig 2).

FIG 3

3 Set the four front boards together (the two doors at centre and a side piece on either side), spring the rule across the top and draw out the curved profile (see Fig 2). Get help if needed. Repeat this procedure for the other end.

FIG 5

5 Take the six 160 mm shelf supports (two to support each shelf, two to support the top of the cupboard and two to support the bottom) and use the mitre saw to cut one end of each piece to 45° (see Fig 5).

FIG 4

4 Take the door (all screwed together) and with the curved ends clearly marked out, very carefully cut the curved profile on the scroll saw (see Fig 4). Cut the two side boards in the same way. Sand the sawn edges to a smooth, slightly rounded and blurred finish.

FIG 6

6 Take the three 312 mm shelf boards and screw the 160 mm shelf supports to the ends, so that the square end of the support is flush with the back edge of the shelf board (see Fig 6). Use the block and sandpaper to rub all edges and ends to a smooth finish.

FIG 7

7 Screw the three shelf boards to the paired side boards (see Fig 7). Note that the middle shelf is placed so that the supports are on the underside, with the mitred ends looking to what will be the front of the cupboard. Screw the other two side boards in place.

FIG 8

8 Screw the four back boards in place, with screws running through into the edges of the shelves and the side boards (see Fig 8). The screws should be flush with the surface. Screw the front of the cupboard in place, this time sinking the holes with the counter-bore bit so that the screws will lie well below the surface.

FIG 9

9 Whittle the three components that make the door catch – the piece that screws to the side of the cupboard, the latch and the central swivel. There is no need to copy the design exactly, just study it to see how it functions and then go for a similar form. Drill through the latch with the 10 mm bit and slide the central swivel in place. Drill a 3 mm hole through the side of the unit and fix with a dowel whittled from an offcut (make it 100 mm long and 3 mm in diameter). Continue carving the catch components until the form becomes a pleasing whole (see Fig 9). Use a fold of sandpaper wrapped around a stick to sculpt the wood to a smooth shape and finish.

FIG 10

10 Set the door in place, spike the screw-holes with the awl and screw the hinges in place. Depending upon the size of your chosen hinges, position one about 140 mm down from the top and the other about 100 mm up from the bottom (see Fig 10). Use a fold of fine-grade sandpaper to blur the surface of the brass hinges and dull the shine.

FIG 11

11 Screw the catch to the side of the cupboard and use it to establish the position of the swivel latch. Mark the pivot point with a pencil, and drill with the 10 mm bit. Slide the central peg in place (see Fig 11). Drill a hole in the peg with the 3 mm bit, on the inside face of the door. Whittle a pin with the knife and slide it through to hold the latch in place.

Rub down all the surfaces with the graded sandpapers. Dilute the paint in water and colour-wash the cupboard. When it is dry, sand all the surfaces to a smooth finish – cutting through the paint to reveal the grain – and wipe all the surfaces with teak oil. With the plug cutter, cut little plugs from scrap wood and glue them in the counter-bored holes to cover the screwheads.

> ## TIP
> It's a good idea to experiment with colourwashing before you tackle the cupboard. Thin some acrylic paint with water and paint a piece of scrap wood, then sand and oil as described. If you want the colour to be lighter or darker, simply add more water or paint accordingly. Remember that sawn edges and light grain absorb more colour and look darker.

Construction variations

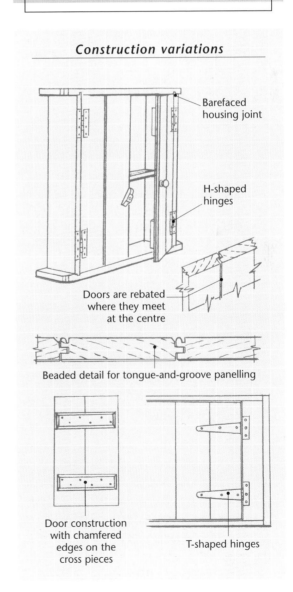

Barefaced housing joint

H-shaped hinges

Doors are rebated where they meet at the centre

Beaded detail for tongue-and-groove panelling

Door construction with chamfered edges on the cross pieces

T-shaped hinges

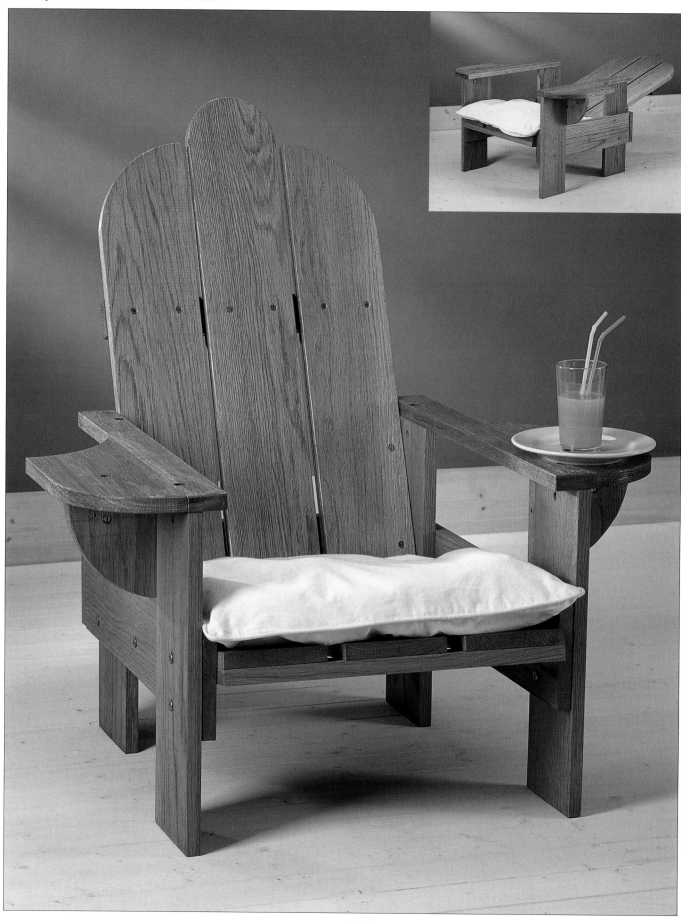

Adjustable porch chair

If you would like to build a swift and easy porch chair, this classic "crate" design is sure to please. The project draws its inspiration from the work of Gerrit Rietveld (1888–1957), the Dutch designer and architect, and member of the De Stijl group, who developed designs that could be made from salvaged wood. It's a stylish chair, perfect for the porch, conservatory or studio. The back can be adjusted. If you want to relax and stretch out for a doze, you simply withdraw the two gate bolts in order to lower the back.

The chair is made from American oak, and the boards are jointed with screws and toggle fasteners. The great thing about the design is that the whole chair can be made without having to cut any joints. The boards are simply butted or sandwiched and then fitted with toggle fasteners running through the thickness. The two H-frames that make up the arms are linked by the seat frame in such a way that the back can be fixed in either an upright or horizontal mode. To finish the surface of the wood, it is vigorously wire-brushed to give it a weathered texture and wiped with Danish oil.

───────────── Essential Tools ─────────────

workbench with vice, compasses, pencil, rule, square, G-clamps, bench drill press, 10 mm and 15 mm forstner bits, 5 mm twist bit, scroll saw, 2 sash clamps, block plane, sanding block, wire brush, paintbrush, pilot-countersink bit, screwdriver, hacksaw, metal file, allen key to fit the hex-heads

OTHER USEFUL TOOLS
cordless screwdriver, power sander, electric drill, dividers, marking knife

Adjustable porch chair

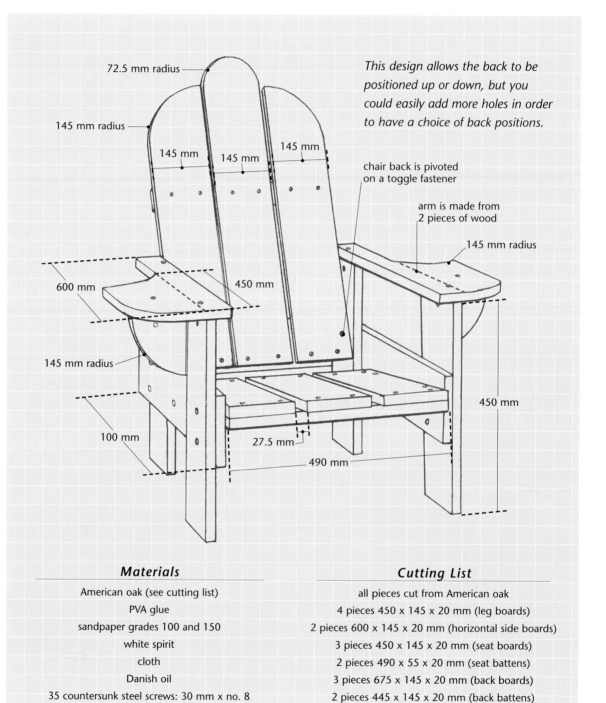

72.5 mm radius

145 mm radius

145 mm

145 mm

145 mm

This design allows the back to be positioned up or down, but you could easily add more holes in order to have a choice of back positions.

chair back is pivoted on a toggle fastener

arm is made from 2 pieces of wood

145 mm radius

600 mm

450 mm

145 mm radius

450 mm

100 mm

27.5 mm

490 mm

Materials

American oak (see cutting list)

PVA glue

sandpaper grades 100 and 150

white spirit

cloth

Danish oil

35 countersunk steel screws: 30 mm x no. 8

16 steel and brass hex-head toggle fasteners complete with threaded steel rod to fit

2 steel gate bolts with screws: to fit a 10 mm hole

Cutting List

all pieces cut from American oak

4 pieces 450 x 145 x 20 mm (leg boards)

2 pieces 600 x 145 x 20 mm (horizontal side boards)

3 pieces 450 x 145 x 20 mm (seat boards)

2 pieces 490 x 55 x 20 mm (seat battens)

3 pieces 675 x 145 x 20 mm (back boards)

2 pieces 445 x 145 x 20 mm (back battens)

2 pieces 600 x 55 x 20 mm (arm battens)

2 pieces 450 x 145 x 20 mm (arm boards)

1 piece 540 x 145 x 20 mm (back frame board)

FIG 1

1 Study the working drawing and work out the position of the various drilled holes. Build a simple jig using workshop offcuts, and clamp the jig to the bench drill press with G-clamps. Set to work drilling the blind holes to fit the brass hex-heads, using the 15 mm forstner bit (see Fig 1). Drill to a depth of 5 mm.

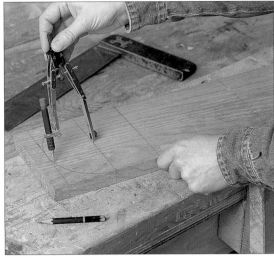

FIG 3

3 Take the three 675 mm back boards, decide on the best ends and faces, and use the compasses to set out the top details. Use a radius of 72.5 mm for the middle board, and 145 mm for the other two (see Fig 3). If you can get hold of an adjustable compass to use, it is better because the legs stay put and will not slip.

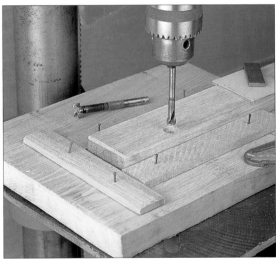

FIG 2

2 Change to the 10 mm forstner bit and continue the hole through the thickness of the wood (see Fig 2). Re-run this procedure for all the hex-head holes. Use the 10 mm forstner bit for the toggle holes, and the 5 mm twist bit for the screw and rod holes.

FIG 4

4 Fit a new fine-toothed blade in the scroll saw, make adjustments to ensure maximum tension, and then fret out the top ends of the three back boards (see Fig 4). If you work at a slow pace, the sawn edge will turn out to be so smooth that it will hardly need sanding.

FIG 5

6 Use the block plane and sandpaper to work the end-grain surfaces of all components to a good finish, chamfering all the corners and edges. Wire-brush all surfaces. Remove the dust with a cloth dampened in white spirit and brush all the surfaces with Danish oil (see Fig 6).

FIG 7

5 Take one of the 450 mm arm boards, set the compasses to a radius of 145 mm and scribe the back end of the board with the quarter-circle curve that makes the design. Fret out the curve on the scroll saw and keep the piece of quarter-circle waste for the arm bracket. Take the fretted arm board and one of the 600 mm arm battens, smear glue on mating side faces and clamp them together with the sash clamps (see Fig 5). Be careful not to over-tighten the clamps so that they buckle. When the glue is dry, scribe an identical quarter-circle curve on the front end of the arm and fret it out on the scroll saw. Re-run this procedure for the other arm.

7 To build the seat, set the two 490 mm seat battens flat on the bench and bridge them with the three 450 mm seat boards. Use a piece of wood 27.5 mm thick to space the boards precisely the same distance apart. Make checks with the square and rule, drill screwholes with the pilot-countersink bit and fix the boards in place with screws (see Fig 7).

FIG 6

TIP

Depending upon the manufacturer, hex-head toggle fasteners come in many shapes, types and sizes. They may be made of stainless steel or plastic rather than brass, and the hex-head size may differ, so you might well need to use a different-size drill bit to suit the particular design and size of your fitting. Buy the fittings and experiment on scrap wood to ascertain the necessary drill size.

FIG 8

FIG 9

9 Screw the arm bracket to the inside edge of the front leg board and fit the arm board with the toggle fasteners (see Fig 9). Repeat on the other arm. Check with the square.

8 To build the side H-frames, take two 450 mm vertical leg boards and bridge them with the 600 mm horizontal side board (with one leg under and the other over). Slide the toggle fasteners in place (hex-heads, toggle and threaded rod cut to length with the hacksaw and tidied up with the file), and use the allen key to tighten up just enough to grip. Make checks with the square, and complete necessary adjustments to the alignment. Clench the toggle fasteners to make the whole thing stable (see Fig 8). Re-run this procedure for the other H-frame. While the two H-frames are identical in every respect, they are also mirror image copies of each other, as are the arms of most chairs.

FIG 10

10 Finally, when you have pivoted the seat back on the toggle fasteners – as shown in the working drawing – and screwed the horizontal back board in place, fix the two gate bolts (see Fig 10).

Construction variations

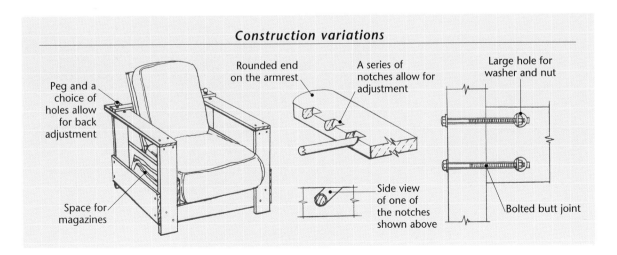

Peg and a choice of holes allow for back adjustment

Space for magazines

Rounded end on the armrest

A series of notches allow for adjustment

Side view of one of the notches shown above

Large hole for washer and nut

Bolted butt joint

Log trough

This design represents a coming together of various trough designs. It is inspired both by a baker's dough trough and an early nineteenth-century washing trough – though the handle owes its shape to a New England knife tray on display at the American Museum in Bath.

This log trough is made from pine and plywood. The fretted handle strip is screwed to the end board, while the sides are nailed to the ends. It's a surprisingly challenging project. If you are interested in building other troughs and need inspiration, visit a rural life museum to see the beautiful troughs used in the house, dairy and garden.

Essential Tools
---

workbench with vice and holdfast, compasses, pencils, rule, square, bevel gauge, bench drill press, 5 mm and 8 mm twist bits, scroll saw, 2 short sash clamps, screwdriver, spokeshave, block plane, router and router table, 10 mm groove cutter, sanding block, medium pin hammer, paintbrush

OTHER USEFUL TOOLS
cordless screwdriver, power sander, electric drill, dividers, marking knife

Log trough

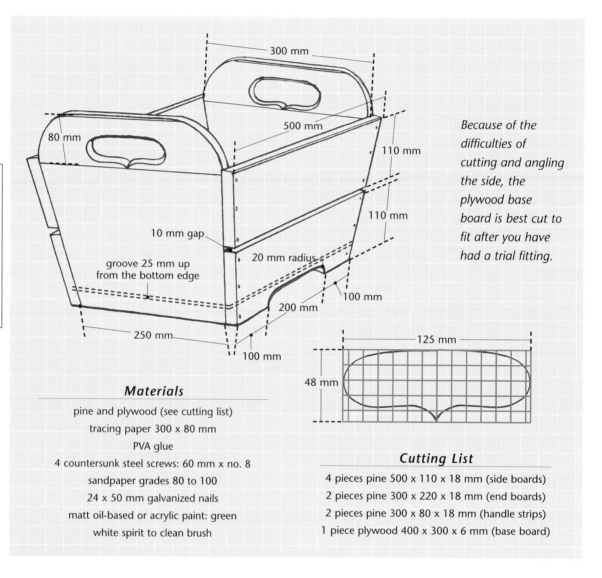

- 300 mm
- 80 mm
- 500 mm
- 110 mm
- 110 mm
- 10 mm gap
- groove 25 mm up from the bottom edge
- 20 mm radius
- 100 mm
- 200 mm
- 250 mm
- 100 mm
- 125 mm
- 48 mm

Because of the difficulties of cutting and angling the side, the plywood base board is best cut to fit after you have had a trial fitting.

You'll need to know

CUTTING CURVED SHAPES
p.16

ROUTING A GROOVE
p.20

NAILING AND PINNING
p.22

Materials

pine and plywood (see cutting list)

tracing paper 300 x 80 mm

PVA glue

4 countersunk steel screws: 60 mm x no. 8

sandpaper grades 80 to 100

24 x 50 mm galvanized nails

matt oil-based or acrylic paint: green

white spirit to clean brush

Cutting List

4 pieces pine 500 x 110 x 18 mm (side boards)

2 pieces pine 300 x 220 x 18 mm (end boards)

2 pieces pine 300 x 80 x 18 mm (handle strips)

1 piece plywood 400 x 300 x 6 mm (base board)

FIG 1

1 Take your piece of tracing paper – the same size as the handle strip – and fold it in half along its length so that the crease becomes the centre-line. Use a soft pencil to carefully draw one half of the shape of the handle on the tracing paper. Establish the centre-lines on the two handle strips. With a hard pencil, press-transfer the shape of the handle through to both pieces of wood. Shade in the waste so that there is no doubting what needs to be cut away (see Fig 1). You might need to adjust the handle to fit your hand.

FIG 2

2 Take the four side boards and use the bevel gauge, rule and square to draw the overall shape of the angled side. Use the rule and compasses to draw the foot detail on the two bottom side boards (see Fig 2).

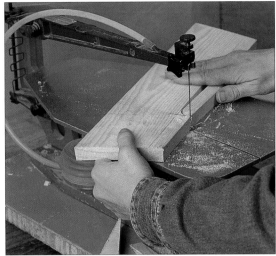

FIG 4

4 Cut out the shape of the side boards on the scroll saw (see Fig 4). Work at a steady pace, cutting to the waste side of the drawn line. Next, cut out the shape of the two end boards. Pencil-label all the component parts.

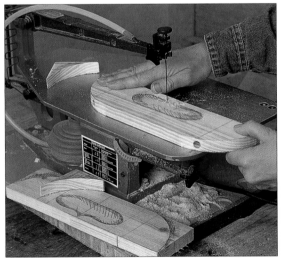

FIG 3

3 Take the handle strips and drill the screwholes. Drill the 5 mm pilot holes completely through the wood, then re-drill the hole with an 8 mm bit to a depth of 30 mm (so the screw can be sunk). Cut out the shape of the handle on the scroll saw. When you come to cut the handle hole, enter and exit the blade where the pointed detail meets the edge (see Fig 3).

FIG 5

5 Take one end board and a fretted handle strip, smear glue on mating edges and clamp up. Drive the screws down the pilot holes and then remove the two clamps (see Fig 5). Repeat this procedure for the other end.

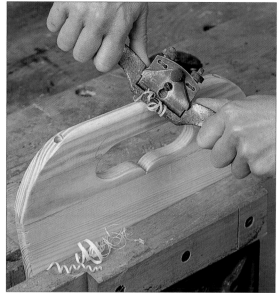

FIG 6

7 Use the block plane, set to a fine cut, to swiftly chamfer all sides and ends of the side boards (see Fig 7). Don't aim for a really exquisite finish – small irregularities are in keeping with the style of the project.

FIG 8

6 When the glue is dry, set the end board in the vice. Use the spokeshave to plane the top edge of the end board to a slightly rounded, smooth finish (see Fig 6). Work from centre to side so you do not split the wood by running the blade into the end grain.

Take a fold of sandpaper and rub the inside edges of the handle hole to a good, smooth finish. Concentrate your efforts on the top of the hole, so the handle is easy and comfortable to hold.

8 Attach the router to its table, fit the 10 mm groove cutter and set the fence to 25 mm. Run the two end boards and the side boards through to cut a groove 10 mm wide and 6 mm deep, 25 mm up from the bottom edge (see Fig 8). Use a push-stick to feed the wood through and keep your fingers out of harm's way.

FIG 7

FIG 9

9 Have a dry run put-together in order to decide (by eye) how much the edges of the two end boards need to be angled back. Then pair the two boards back to back in the vice, and use the block plane to angle back from the mating faces (see Fig 9).

FIG 10

10 Trim the plywood base board to fit your trough. Give all the component parts a swift rub-down with sandpaper, then start nailing the whole thing together (see Fig 10). As the nailing progresses, you will see that the side and end boards cant (lean) out to the extent that the 6 mm-thick plywood base becomes a tight fit in the 10 mm-wide grooves.

You might even need to ease the base by chamfering the edges of the routed grooves slightly. When the whole box is nailed together, give it a coat of paint on all surfaces.

When the paint is completely dry, sand selected faces and edges to cut through the paint. Concentrate your efforts on areas that would, in the normal course of events, receive most wear.

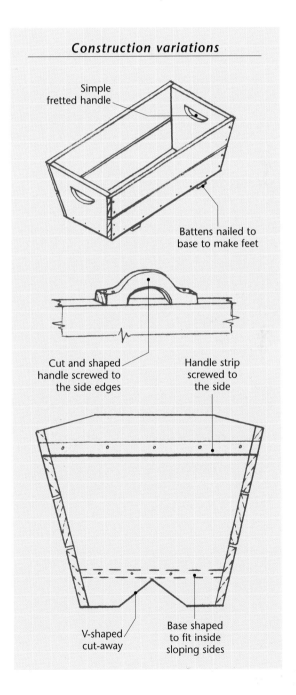

Construction variations

Simple fretted handle

Battens nailed to base to make feet

Cut and shaped handle screwed to the side edges

Handle strip screwed to the side

V-shaped cut-away

Base shaped to fit inside sloping sides

Child's bed

This simple design uses low-cost materials, and a minimum skill level is required for the joints involved. The use of a router is recommended to cut the headboard housings. Although they can be cut by hand, it is a time-consuming business and a router will give you a far more professional finish.

The headboard and footboard could easily be adapted to your child's personal taste – for example, the headboard cut-out could be a silhouette of a favourite cartoon character; use a photocopier to enlarge a drawing and then paint the headboard to suit.

Before starting, take into account the size of mattress you will be using. All of the measurements for this bed are designed to fit a 2 m-long by 800 mm-wide mattress. If your mattress is a different size, you will have to adapt the measurements.

This bed is finished with a semi-matt paint applied on top of primer and undercoat, but you could use a colour wash or stain, or just varnish. Gloss paint could soon look tatty, however.

Essential Tools

pencil, straightedge, tape, square, marking gauge, screwdriver, tenon saw, jigsaw, electric drill, 12 mm flat bit, 3 mm twist bit, 8 mm wood bit, 6 mm multi-speed bit (200 mm long), 12 and 25 mm bevel-edge chisels, mallet, block plane, workbench, two sash cramps or two pairs of slow folding wedges

OTHER USEFUL TOOLS
mortise gauge, table-mounted circular saw, router with 12 mm straight cutter

Child's bed

The dimensions of this bed make it suitable for a child of up to about 14 or 15 years old. As with many of the other projects in this book, you can adapt the dimensions and lists of materials to suit your own requirements.

You'll need to know

PREPARING WOOD p. 16

ROUTING pp. 19–21

SAWS pp. 6–10

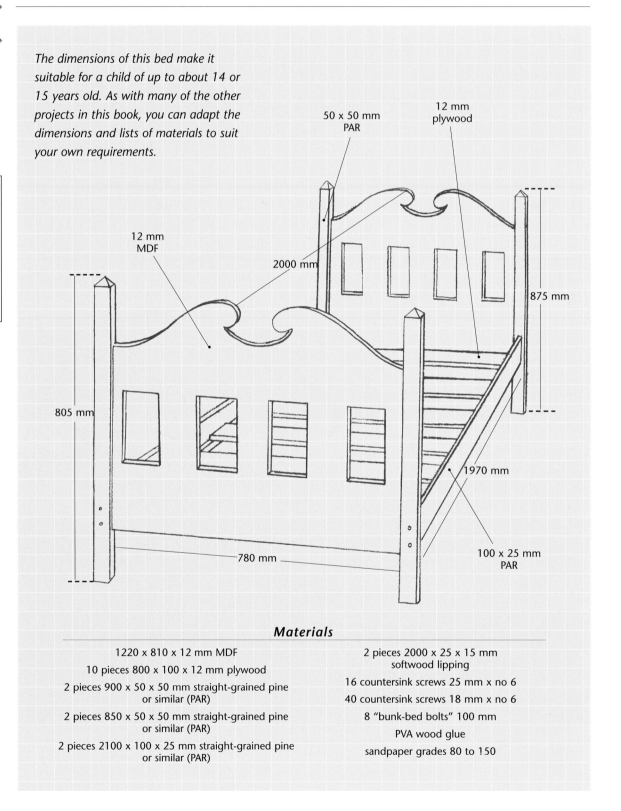

50 x 50 mm PAR

12 mm plywood

12 mm MDF

2000 mm

875 mm

805 mm

1970 mm

780 mm

100 x 25 mm PAR

Materials

1220 x 810 x 12 mm MDF

10 pieces 800 x 100 x 12 mm plywood

2 pieces 900 x 50 x 50 mm straight-grained pine or similar (PAR)

2 pieces 850 x 50 x 50 mm straight-grained pine or similar (PAR)

2 pieces 2100 x 100 x 25 mm straight-grained pine or similar (PAR)

2 pieces 2000 x 25 x 15 mm softwood lipping

16 countersink screws 25 mm x no 6

40 countersink screws 18 mm x no 6

8 "bunk-bed bolts" 100 mm

PVA wood glue

sandpaper grades 80 to 150

FIG 1

FIG 2

1 For the legs, you need two 900 mm and two 850 mm lengths of 50 x 50 mm timber. Lay all four lengths side by side, with the best face uppermost and one end of all four legs aligned. Mark these faces as your face sides. Lay a square as near to the end of the four legs as you can and draw a line across all of them. This is the base line of the legs, which will then need to be squared around each leg. Measure 205 mm from this line and draw another line across all four legs, to represent the bottom of the mortise for the side rails to enter. At this point you will need to measure accurately the true width of the 100 x 25 mm dimensioned timber, normally about 92 mm. Transfer this measurement to the legs so that the third line will be the width of the side rails along from the second line you drew. Transfer these two lines to the backs of the legs. Set your mortise gauge to 12 mm between the pins, 15 mm from the stock to the nearest pin. Then mark as shown in Fig 1.

2 Separate the legs into two pairs and mark them left and right. On the inner face of each pair, mark out for the housings into which the headboard and footboard will fit. For the headboard mark a line 520 mm from the base line, and for the footboard a line 450 mm. Leave the pins of the mortise gauge set to 12 mm, but adjust the stock to 15 mm, and mark as shown in Fig 2.

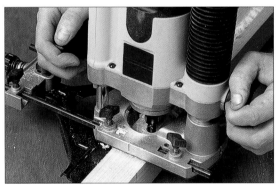

FIG 3

3 Clamp each leg to the bench, and use a router with a side fence to groove out the side channels to a depth of 15 mm (Fig 3). Turn each leg over and remove the mortise for the rails to a depth of 18 mm. Mark the full height of each leg – for the head pair this is 875 mm, and for the foot pair it is 805 mm. To finish the tops of the legs with a pyramid shape, measure 50 mm back from the top on each leg and make a 45-degree cut on all four sides. Cut the bottom of the legs to the line you first drew as the base line in step 1.

TIP

Bunk-bed bolts might be difficult to locate, so track them down before you begin. You should be able to obtain them from a good hardware supplier, who will be able to order them if they are not in stock. Look in your Yellow Pages or local telephone directory under "Hardware Retailers".

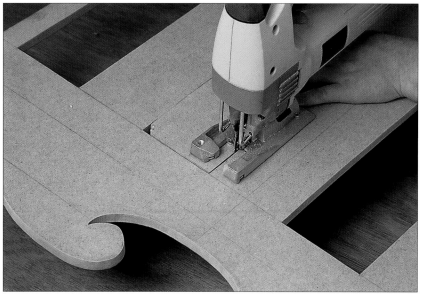

FIG 4

TIP

When drilling the holes for the bunk-bed bolts in the legs, you will find it easier and more efficient if you place the bed on the floor with one end pressed up against a wall.

4 From the 810 mm edge of the MDF (medium-density fibreboard) sheet measure 580 mm square across and cut the board into two pieces; the smaller is the footboard. Working from the template on page 253, cut out the shape using a jigsaw fitted with a scrolling blade for the curves and a normal blade for the straight lines (see Fig 4). Repeat for the headboard, but remember to extend the template so that the overall height is 650 mm. Assemble each set of legs and board together and glue up, using sash cramps or slow folding wedges to hold the pieces in position.

5 Now take the two rails and cut them to a length of 2036 mm. Choose your face sides, turn them over and mark out for a stub tenon 18 mm long and 12 mm thick at each end. Use a tenon saw and a chisel to remove the waste, as shown in Fig 5. Next cut the two pieces of 25 x 15 mm softwood lipping to length and glue and screw them to the bottom of the rails using the 25 mm x no. 6 gauge screws. Wipe away any excess glue before it has a chance to dry, and assemble the rails to the head and foot-board assemblies.

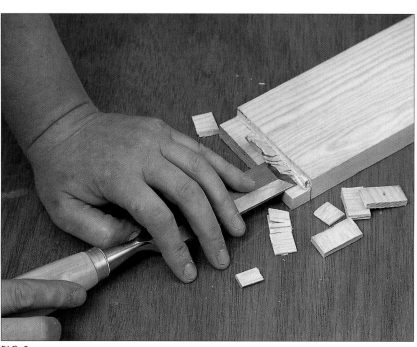

FIG 5

FIG 6

FIG 7

6 The two lines transferred in step 1 enable you to line up the bolts with the tenons. Find the centre of the legs and drill two holes evenly spaced with the 6 mm bit. Drill through the leg, through the tenon and into the rail, keeping the drill square to the leg (Fig 6). Use tape as a depth gauge on the bit so that you only drill the length of the bolts. Repeat this process on the other three legs.

FIG 8

7 Once the bed is assembled you will now have to insert the cylindrical nuts for the bunk-bed bolts. This can be a little tricky to get right because, no matter how careful you have been to keep your drill square in step 6, some error will almost certainly have occurred. For ease of explanation, this step is shown in more detail (see Fig 7). Insert the bolts into the holes, leaving about 30 mm protruding. Use a square or a straightedge to sight the top and bottom of each bolt, then draw two sets of parallel lines and make a mark across them about 10 mm short of the length of the bolts. Drill an 8 mm hole through this mark to receive the cylindrical nut. Insert the nuts and screw up the bolts, but be careful not to over-tighten them at this stage.

8 Cut the plywood slats to the length required and lay them across the two pieces of lipping. Pre-drill and countersink each one, then glue and screw them into place using two 18 mm x no 6 screws at both ends of each slat (see Fig 8). The end slats should be 50 mm from the headboard and footboard, with a 100 mm gap between all the others.

Chair and footstool

This style of sturdy and extremely comfortable patio chair is common throughout North America, where it is called an Adirondack chair, the name deriving from the range of mountains in upstate New York. All the timbers are simply screwed and glued together, using no joints. Start by making the footstool and, when you have gained confidence, tackle the chair.

It is possible to construct this chair from almost any timber, even 18 mm exterior-grade or marine plywood. If cost is of little concern, teak or iroko would be superb. Secondhand mahogany is used here.

If you feel that the sloping back of the chair is beyond your capabilities, make the chair with a 90-degree back and straight slats screwed to the back of the final seating slat, which would be straight, as opposed to the curved one shown here. To finish, a two-part epoxy coating is used here. This is expensive and tricky to apply, but once wood is properly coated with epoxy, it becomes totally stable and virtually maintenance-free. Stains, polyurethane varnish and gloss paint are acceptable for the finish, but you will have to revarnish or paint your chair every four or five summers.

Essential Tools

pencil, straightedge, tape, square, marking gauge, sliding bevel, string, screwdriver, tenon saw, panel saw, jigsaw, electric drill, 3 mm, 4 mm, 6 mm and 8 mm wood bits, size 8 plug cutter, block plane, jack plane, workbench

OTHER USEFUL TOOLS
belt sander, palm sander, beam compass, spokeshave

Chair and footstool

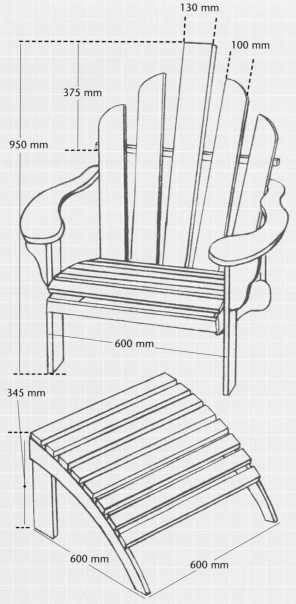

**You'll need
to know**

PREPARING WOOD
p. 16

PLANING
p. 18

SAWS
pp. 6–10

Materials

FOOTSTOOL
9 pieces 600 x 50 x 25 mm (slats)
2 pieces 600 x 150 x 25 mm (side rails)
2 pieces 300 x 100 x 25 mm (legs)
36 zinc-plated countersink screws 38 mm x no 8
2 brass bolts 65 x 6 mm with nuts and washers

CHAIR
8 pieces 600 x 50 x 25 mm (seat slats)
2 pieces 900 x 150 x 25 mm (side rails)
2 pieces 500 x 100 x 25 mm (legs)
2 pieces 200 x 100 x 25 mm (arm rest brackets)
2 pieces 750 x 200 x 25 mm (arm rests)
700 x 170 x 25 mm (curved seat slat/back joining rib)
2 pieces 600 x 90 x 25 mm (back braces)
2 pieces 620 x 100 x 25 mm (outer back slats)
2 pieces 730 x 100 x 25 mm (inner back slats)
850 x 130 x 25 mm (centre back slat)
700 x 50 x 50 mm (strengthening blocks)
200 zinc-plated countersink screws 38 mm x no 8
40 zinc-plated countersink screws 45 mm x no 8
4 brass bolts 65 x 6 mm with nuts and washers
epoxy wood glue (system 106 or equivalent)
sandpaper grades 80 to 300

*An alternative design for these chairs and
stools is to use mortise and tenon joints; the
method here is just as sturdy – and easier!*

FOOTSTOOL

1 The upper and lower radii of the stool rails are 750 mm, with the centres taken from two different positions. Set this out first on some scrap ply or paper first. Draw a line 570 mm long, divide it in half and draw a line 55 mm at right angles to the centre. Extend the line back along

the 55 mm until it is 750 mm in total. This is the position of your first centre. Set your beam compass or string and pencil accordingly and strike the upper arc (see Fig 1). Where the arc touches the 570 mm line, square off 38 mm at one end and 75 mm at the other. These two new lines give you

FIG 1

FIG 2

the position of the second centre by simply scribing an arc at 750 mm from the end of each line; where the arcs intersect is the second centre point. Cut out the shape with a jigsaw and use it as a template for the other rail. Do not cut to the 38 mm line, but leave the rail overlong at this stage. Lay each rail over the leg section, clamp them together and rest on a flat surface. Mark the base line of the rail by scribing from the table, cut and check. Mark and cut any overhang at the wider end of the rail, which needs to finish flush with the back edge of the vertical leg.

2 When you are happy that the assembly sits flat on the surface, drill and bolt the two parts together; do not overtighten. Next cut out all the slats, rounding the first slat if you wish. When they are all cut to length and arrised, lay them out together and mark out for the screw holes. Come in half the width of a rail from the end of each slat, and mark two equidistant screw holes for each end of each slat. With an 8 mm bit, drill down about 5 mm for the plugs, then drill through with a 4 mm bit for the screw shank (see Fig 2).

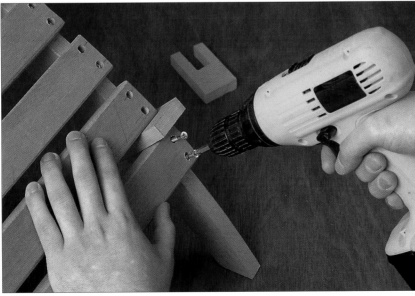

FIG 3

3 Fix all the slats in place one by one, 15 mm apart, using two MDF or ply spacers, drilling through the screw shank hole into the rails with a 3 mm pilot hole (see Fig 3). Fix one slat at a time and check that the two rails remain parallel and that you are fixing the slats square to the rails. Do not drive the screws fully home or glue up.

4 From offcuts matching the footstool, cut a sufficient number of plugs to fill the screw holes, using a guide for the plug cutter clamped to the wood (see Fig 4). The guide can be made from 6 mm MDF (medium-density fibreboard) or plywood. When you have enough plugs, disassemble the stool and position the screws, nuts and bolts to hand. Ensure that the work area is dust-free and prepare to glue up (refer to step 15 for details). Before driving in the screws during final assembly, rub each screw thread against a wax candle or some beeswax to drive them home with far less effort.

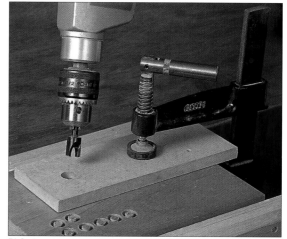

FIG 4

CHAIR

FIG 5

TIP

When using countersink screws, make the counterbore into the timber about 5 mm deep; any less, and you will find it difficult to cut the plugs accurately.

5 Draw out the rails freehand onto the 900 x 150 mm lengths. Use the full length, and make sure that the rails are not less than 100 mm wide at any point. The height at the front of the chair rail should match the height of the back of the footstool (about 300 mm). As you have already done for the stool, scribe the back to the bench top while the leg is clamped in position but this time, instead of cutting the front end of the rail flush to the leg, let it project forward about 100 mm and round it off. Mark the position of the leg on the rail and unclamp. Mark two flats on the front that you have drawn; these will take the front two rails, the uppermost needing to be 15 mm forward of the front of the leg. Draw the flat 50 mm, add another 15 mm gap, and then draw the second 50 mm flat (see Fig 5). Cut this out with a jigsaw and copy the shape to its pair. Finish off to a smooth surface with a belt sander and bolt the legs to the rails.

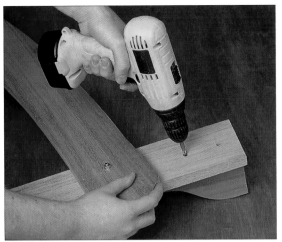

FIG 6

FIG 8

6 The top of the legs will now need to be marked and drilled for the arm rest brackets (see Fig 6). Remember to drill for the plugs first, then the shank. Drill the pilot holes when you assemble. The brackets can be a simple triangle or a little more ornate; you will get both brackets from one short length. Assemble the seat slats as in steps 2 and 3.

7 When marking out the curvature of the final seat slat, the most effective method is to use a steel rule as shown in Fig 7. As you increase the pressure at either end of the rule, you can alter the ellipse of the curve: equal pressure gives an equal curve. The timber you use should be wide enough to leave an off-cut of about 50 mm at its narrowest point; this will form the reinforcing rib behind the back. When you have decided on the amount of curvature you want for the back slats, mark and cut with a jigsaw.

8 Drill the holes for screwing the final slat to the rails and mark the centre line. Now position a flat across the curve 50 mm each side of the centre line, then use the slat spacer to mark a gap of 15 mm and after that a further 100 mm flat, as shown in Fig 8. The actual back slats from this chair are used here as a guide from which to mark off, prior to shaping them, rather than separate guide ones. Plane to the lines of the flats and then clamp them in place on the seat assembly, checking slats and rails for square.

FIG 7

FIG 9

9 Position the offcut left over from step 7 by using the spacers, 15 mm away from the clamped slat. Use a small offcut about 25 mm thick to transfer the flats to form the front profile of the reinforcing rail for the back slats (see Fig 9). Cut to the scribed lines with a jigsaw.

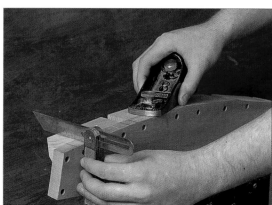

FIG 10

10 Unclamp the final slat from the assembly and then screw five strengthening blocks, each of them about 90 mm long, to the underside, to give an added glue area to the base of the back slats. Any strong hardwood will do for the strengthening blocks; offcuts of beech are used here. Screw the blocks from underneath to the rear of the final rail, running along each flat. Plane them flush using a block or a jack plane to achieve a consistent bevel of about 85 degrees, as shown in Fig 10.

11 Place the final slat edge down on the work bench and lay out the five pre-cut slats that form the back. The two 620 mm long back slats are placed at the outside, then the 730 mm slats, with the longest at 850 mm, placed in the middle. Try to get an even distance between each slat at the top. Position the offcut from step 7 about two-thirds of the way along the back to form a rib. This takes trial and error; you may find you have to reduce or increase the splay of the back, or lengthen the flats on the rib. When the fit is acceptable, mark the back slats where the rib sits and set aside. Mark each slat for the top profile and the bottom angle. Cut to fit with a jigsaw. Copy the top detail from the photograph on page 146, if you wish.

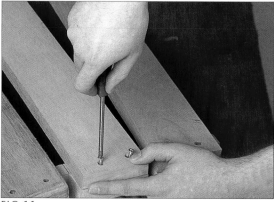

FIG 11

12 When cut, drill and screw together and place the assembly back on the rails. At this stage the back is fragile and will flop about, so take care. Check the fit of the rib again and, if good, drill through the back slats, two holes per slat, taking great care that the drill does not burst through the face of the rib. Screw the rib and back slat temporarily in place to provide some rigidity – every other screw hole will be sufficient at this stage (see Fig 11). From the narrowest point of the rib draw a smooth line that follows the curvature of the back to each end. Draw a half-round to finish level with the two end back slats. Remove, cut the waste with a jigsaw, sand or plane smooth, then refit.

FIG 12

FIG 13

FIG 14

13 Fit the two braces that support the back underneath the back rib. Bolt them to the inside of the back of the rails. Leave the bottom width of the braces at 90 mm and taper the upper end so that it is the same width as the rib. Cut the bottom as a half-round and the top as a compound mitre, meeting the back face of the outer back slat and the underside of the rib (see Fig 13 for detail). Mark the compound mitre by scribing from the relevant faces, and use a sharp block plane to plane down to the lines (Fig 12). When correctly shaped, drill and screw the top in place and use a bolt to fix the brace to the bottom to the rail.

TIP

When gluing up, cover your workbench with newspaper to catch any drips of adhesive.

---

14 The key factors influencing the shape of the arms are: at the front, you need enough space for a large gin and tonic, and the back needs to curl around the outside of the outer edge of the outer back slat and butt up to the outer face of the braces. The best way to achieve this is to use an offcut of MDF or ply and obtain the shape by a process of trial and error (see Fig 14). Use a spirit level to position the arms, then mark the underside where it meets the brace. Fit a small block at this mark and then screw the arm down onto the block. The front of the arm is screwed down into the front leg and arm rest bracket. When gluing up, pour a little glue into these holes as you are screwing into end grain.

15 When applying epoxy resin, use rubber gloves, mix accurately according to the manufacturer's instructions, and work quickly – drips and spillage can be cleaned off later. Mix only as much glue as you can use in 25 minutes. Glue the legs, rails and slats together, screwing and bolting as you go, then mix a further amount for the plugs. Leave to cure for a day, then clean off any excess glue with a chisel and sandpaper and cut the plugs flush.

Shelving unit

A fundamental of good kitchen design is the rule of conceal and display: conceal the unattractive, and display – with verve – the attractive!

This shape works best when hung between two ordinary wall units. It breaks up the rigid lines of most fitted kitchens and allows the eye to be caught by the display. The unit is designed to complement the kitchen sink and wall unit on page 242. Use 12 mm board for the shelf dividers, as the difference in the thickness between the dividers and the 15 mm shelves provides a balance that works well visually. Note also that the end of the front curve passes in front of the sides; this is a bit of a fiddle to mark out, but it will give your shelves a far slicker look.

As always, wear a face mask when working with MDF (medium-density fibreboard), especially when working with power tools. The finish used here is eggshell paint but you could use emulsion, maybe picking out the leading edge of the shelves in a complementary tone, finishing with matt varnish.

Essential Tools

pencil, steel rule or tape, square, string, panel saw, router with 12 mm and 15 mm straight cutters, jigsaw, face mask, drill, 3 mm twist bit, screwdrivers, 12 mm bevel-edge chisel, mallet, jack plane, 2 sash cramps or cramp heads, two 300 mm G-cramps, workbench

OTHER USEFUL TOOLS
beam compass, circular saw, cordless screwdriver, belt sander

Shelving unit

You'll need to know

PREPARING WOOD
p. 16

ROUTING
pp. 19–21

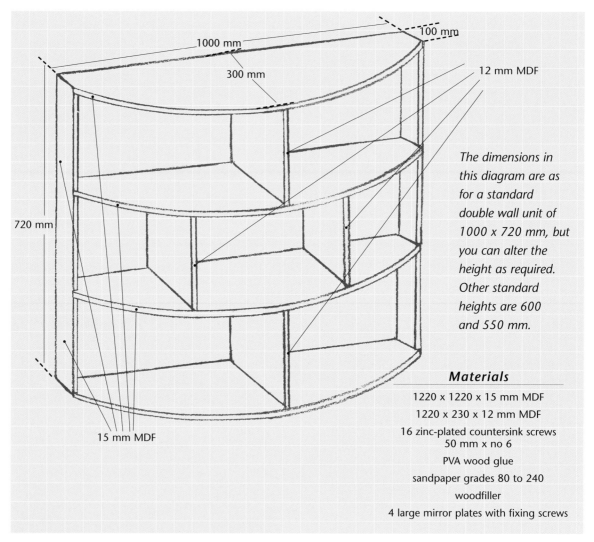

1000 mm

100 mm

300 mm

12 mm MDF

720 mm

15 mm MDF

The dimensions in this diagram are as for a standard double wall unit of 1000 x 720 mm, but you can alter the height as required. Other standard heights are 600 and 550 mm.

Materials

1220 x 1220 x 15 mm MDF

1220 x 230 x 12 mm MDF

16 zinc-plated countersink screws
50 mm x no 6

PVA wood glue

sandpaper grades 80 to 240

woodfiller

4 large mirror plates with fixing screws

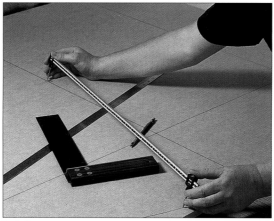

FIG 1

1 Measure 1000 mm from the best MDF edge along two sides of the board. Join the marks, find the centre, mark the top and bottom, and draw a further line parallel to the first. Draw a line 300 mm from the front of the board at 90 degrees to the other two lines. This line should stop at the 1000 mm line drawn first. Use a beam compass or string and pencil to scribe a 720 mm radius arc (see Fig 1); the distance from the outer edge of the arc to the back of the shelf should be 100 mm. Cut, leaving the line on the larger piece, then true up with your plane.

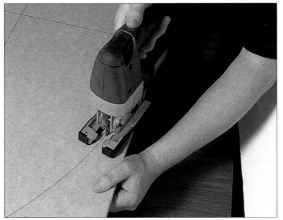

FIG 2

2 Use a jigsaw to cut away the waste from the front of your shelf, making sure that the work is well supported and that there is no likelihood of your cutting into the work-bench (see Fig 2). Use a hand saw or a circular saw to cut the back of this first shelf, and plane or sand the edges as true as you can. This shelf will now be your pattern for the other three and should be marked up accordingly in the steps below.

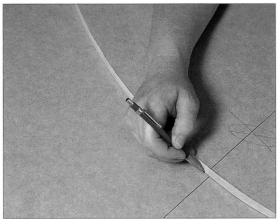

FIG 3

3 Lay the shelf back on the board, ensuring that the centre line is in line with the centre line drawn on the board at both the front and back (see Fig 3). The ends should also be in the correct place. Carefully draw around your pattern shelf. Repeat steps 2 and 3 for the remaining shelves.

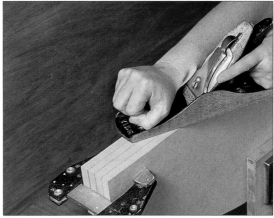

FIG 4

4 Place all four shelves together in your vice, ensuring that the centre line that you drew in step 1 is showing on the front and back of the two outside shelves. Clamp the ends in such a way that you do not interrupt the passage of your plane, and then plane the back edges flat, as shown in Fig 4.

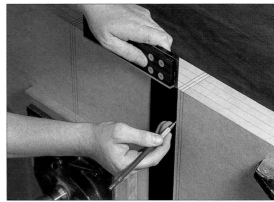

FIG 5

5 You will now need to mark the housings for the uprights. You need three lines, first the centre line already visible; transfer this across the backs of all four shelves. Next, measure out from the centre line 250 mm to both the left and right. Draw a line across the backs, squaring the line down the faces of the two outer shelves. Finally, measure 6 mm on either side of all three lines. Square these marks across the backs and down the front of the outer shelves (see Fig 5).

FIG 6

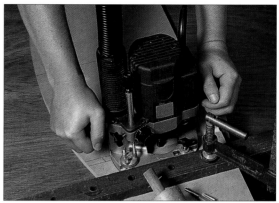

FIG 7

6 Keeping the cramps in place, release the shelves from the vice and turn them around with the curved front edges uppermost. Finish these edges with a belt sander or a sharp plane, working from each end towards the middle. As you work, check the front edges for square, correcting as necessary (see Fig 6). Release the shelves from the vice and cramps. Mark each shelf to identify it: "top", "upper middle", "lower middle" and "bottom". The top shelf has one centrally placed housing on the underside; mark it accordingly. The upper middle shelf has one housing on the top in the centre but two offset on its underside; use one of the shelves that were on the outside when they were in the vice, as they will already have the two outer housings marked on it. Finally set your marking gauge to 20 mm and run it across the front end of each housing. The housings are "stopped housings", so you will not see them from the front when the unit is assembled.

7 Set up your router to cut a 12 mm housing to a depth of 5 mm, and use a fence clamped to the shelf (see Fig 7). Make sure that the cramp is firmly fixed and will not move, then run the router along the fence until you reach the mark made by the marking gauge in step 6. Repeat for each housing on all the shelves.

FIG 8

8 Now cut the ends of your shelves to allow the front edge to pass over the front edge of the sides. For the middle two shelves the process is to mark a line 15 mm in from each end, square from the back of the shelves, then a second line square from the point where the arc meets the end. Remove this 100 x 15 mm portion with a hand- or jigsaw. Repeat the marking-out on the underside of the top shelf and on the top of the bottom shelf. Remove these two portions with the router to a depth of 5 mm, using a 15 mm cutter and a fence set up as before; stop when you reach the line from the end of the arc (see Fig 8).

TIPS

To ensure that you have measured the correct distance from the edge of your router baseplate to the fence, do a test cut on a piece of waste before starting to cut in earnest. To check the alignment, run the router over the cut with the cutter lowered and the motor switched off.

FIG 9

9 Clean up the stopped ends with a sharp chisel. Retrieve the offcut from step 1, then mark it twice to 100 x 710 mm for the sides. Cut the offcut and run a plane over the saw cuts to tidy them up. Next take the 12 mm MDF and cut the uprights: two at 300 x 230 mm and two at 260 x 230 mm. Mark and cut the waste for the stopped housings as shown in Fig 9, to 5 mm deep and 20 mm long on the top and bottom of each upright. (The 230 mm is the height.)

10 Clear your workbench and lay the shelves out in order on their back edges. One by one place the uprights in place, the deeper uprights in the centre of the top and bottom shelves, and the shallow ones off-set between the two middle shelves. Place the side panels in place and get the whole assembly approximately square. Fix a batten down to the bench to hold the bottom shelf in place, fix another batten about 30 mm away from and parallel to the top shelf, then push a set of folding wedges in place. Repeat for the sides. Place your cramps and folding wedges in position with scrap wood as protection, and use them to pull everything into square. If the backs of the shelves are not sitting tight up against the uprights, use an offcut to force them together. When everything fits and is square, mark the centres of the shelf ends where they meet the sides.

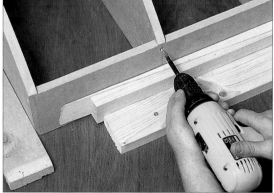

FIG 10

11 Dismantle the assembly, square down from the marks on the side panels and drill two 3 mm holes in each line. Apply PVA glue to all joints, including the shelf ends, and reassemble. Replace the cramps, wedges and offcuts, recheck for square both internally and externally, and drive the 50 mm screws into the holes drilled in the side panels (see Fig 10).

FIG 11

12 Wipe away excess glue with a damp rag (see Fig 11), leave overnight to dry, and then release the wedges and cramps. If any screws are not driven below the surface, withdraw them, countersink the holes and drive them in again. Fill over the screw heads with filler, then plane the front of the uprights to suit the arc of the shelves, planing towards the centre. Finally, sand the edges and the filler over the screws, and paint as required. Use two mirror plates on each of the top and bottom shelves to fix the unit to the wall.

Bathroom accessories

These pieces are designed as a hardwood starter project. You need some basic skills, but not necessarily to have worked with hardwoods before. The project allows you to practise the skill of getting timber perfectly flat and of an even thickness using hand tools. It also introduces the cabinet scraper, an essential tool for obtaining a smooth surface on hardwoods. A biscuit jointer is used for the soap dish and the toothbrush holder; one can be hired for the weekend at a reasonable cost, although once you have used it and appreciated its time-saving versatility, you will want to purchase one.

Burr maple is used for the fittings and plain maple for the duckboard. Virtually any timber could be used – see what your local timber merchant has in stock – but please don't use pine, as it is the quality of the timber used that makes this set of accessories look so attractive. You must use water-resistant glue for this project, as all the items will be subject to the damp atmosphere of the bathroom. The finish is a natural beeswax polish.

Essential Tools

pencil, compasses, tape, square, crosscut saw, jigsaw
with scroll blade, electric drill, 10 mm, 6 mm and
3 mm wood bits, biscuit jointer and 5 size 20 biscuits,
coping saw, half-round file, 12 mm bevel-edge chisel,
jack plane, block plane, cabinet scraper, workbench

OTHER USEFUL TOOLS
table-mounted circular saw

Bathroom accessories

Your fittings may be a different size or proportion to these, in which case adapt the sizes. The only important thing is that there should be a visual balance between the fittings and the wood.

You'll need to know

PLANING
p. 18

SAWS
pp. 6–10

BISCUIT JOINTER
pp. 8

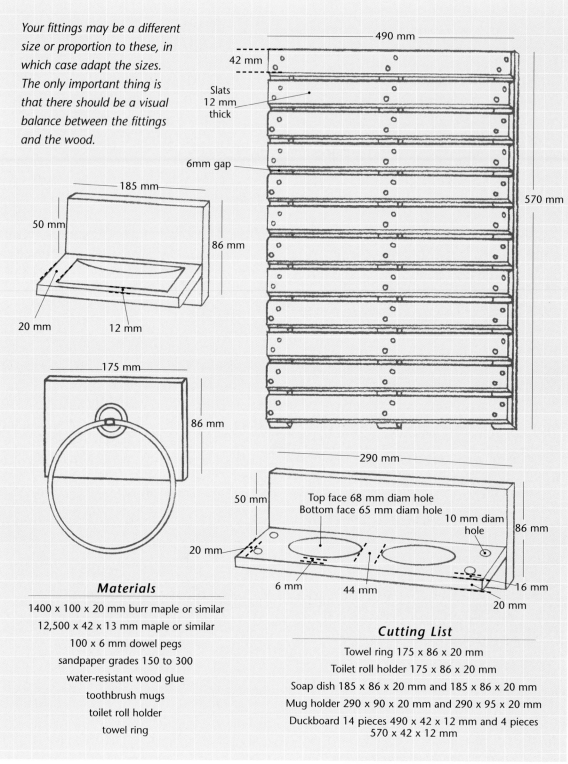

490 mm

42 mm

Slats 12 mm thick

6mm gap

570 mm

185 mm

50 mm

86 mm

20 mm   12 mm

175 mm

86 mm

290 mm

50 mm

Top face 68 mm diam hole
Bottom face 65 mm diam hole

10 mm diam hole

86 mm

20 mm

6 mm   44 mm

16 mm

20 mm

Materials

1400 x 100 x 20 mm burr maple or similar

12,500 x 42 x 13 mm maple or similar

100 x 6 mm dowel pegs

sandpaper grades 150 to 300

water-resistant wood glue

toothbrush mugs

toilet roll holder

towel ring

Cutting List

Towel ring 175 x 86 x 20 mm

Toilet roll holder 175 x 86 x 20 mm

Soap dish 185 x 86 x 20 mm and 185 x 86 x 20 mm

Mug holder 290 x 90 x 20 mm and 290 x 95 x 20 mm

Duckboard 14 pieces 490 x 42 x 12 mm and 4 pieces
570 x 42 x 12 mm

TOILET ROLL HOLDER AND TOWEL RING

FIG 1

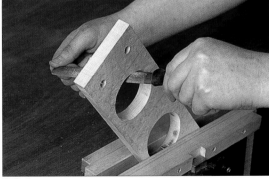

FIG 2

1 Cut two lengths as per the cutting list, then use a sharp jack plane to get the best face of your blocks perfectly flat (see Fig 1). Once flat, plane the best edge true and square to the first face, then mark with face and edge marks. Set a marking gauge to 20 mm and mark around the edges, then plane the other face down to the marks. Aim for fine shavings and plane with the direction of the grain at all times. When both faces are flat and parallel to each other, set your marking gauge to 86 mm, mark for the other edge and plane down to that edge.

2 When the blocks are both accurately sized, use a block plane to remove the arris around the face sides, as shown in Fig 2. Take care that you do not cause splitting when you plane across the end grain; to avoid this, plane from both ends towards the centre. You may find a sharp chisel the best method for the corners.

3 Finish off the front face with a cabinet scraper, then pre-drill pilot holes and screw on the fittings.

TOOTHBRUSH AND MUG HOLDER

FIG 3

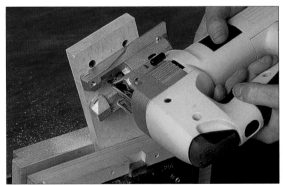

FIG 4

4 Prepare the timbers and mark out for the fittings. To determine the size of the holes for the tapered mugs measure the diameters of the top and the base of the mug, halve the difference between the two diameters and then add that figure to the base diameter. Draw the

circles with a compass and drill a 10 mm hole in the centre for the jigsaw scroll blade (see Fig 3). Use a half-round file or rasp to clean up the jigsaw cut and to introduce the bevel needed to grip the mugs, as shown in Fig 4. Take your time and test the fit of each mug as you go.

FIG 5

5 On the back piece, mark a line about 25 mm from the bottom and run this line along the length of the back. Lay the shelf part against the back and draw three lines on both sections; these will be used as registration marks for the biscuit jointer. One line needs to be in the centre, and the other two should be approximately 50 mm in from each end. Use the biscuit jointer to cut the slots with the work held in the vice (see Fig 5). Check for fit with the biscuits in place and then glue up.

SOAP DISH

FIG 6

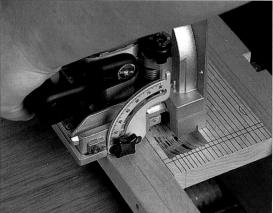
FIG 7

6 Prepare the timber as step 1, then mark out the face side as Fig 6. The multiple lines on the wood are guides for the biscuit jointer to cut out the dish by means of multiple grooves. The lines that run across the width are to line up with the registration marks on the footplate of the jointer.

7 If you are nervous about cutting slots accurately, practise on scrap timber first, and remember to travel in the direction of the blade, i.e. from left to right (Fig 7). Use the lines to keep the tool square, and never plunge the tool into the work until the blade has achieved full speed.

8 The width of the dish allows you to use the end of a cabinet scraper to achieve a perfect finish (see Fig 8) – take care that the corners of the scraper do not cut into the sides of the dish. To fit the biscuits back in place, repeat step 5 as described for the toothbrush and mug holder, although this time you will only need two biscuits, owing to the shorter length of the soap dish.

FIG 8

DUCKBOARD

FIG 9

FIG 10

9 Prepare all the lengths and lay out two long pieces with two short ones on top at the ends to make a frame. Get the four corners square and then clamp the pieces to the bench. To drill for the dowel pegs use a 6 mm drill with a tape mark as a depth gauge, as shown in Fig 9. You do not want to drill all the way through both pieces, but stop the hole about halfway through the lower piece. Drill two holes on each corner and insert pegs into the holes. The frame will now be rigid, allowing you to place the other slats equally spaced apart. Repeat the drilling at all points.

10 Cut off the protruding pegs with a coping saw (see Fig 10), cutting as close as you can but taking care not to scratch the surface. Mark the planks then disassemble, keeping each peg in its correct hole. Glue up and clamp by using lengths of stout timber clamped at each end to make a sandwich.

11 Finally use a sharp chisel to remove any excess glue from the pegs, as shown in Fig 11. You should finish the duckboard with a perfectly smooth surface, achieved by using the cabinet scraper.

TIP

When you are cutting a circular hole with a jigsaw, do not cut right up to the line. The blade can waver and you may make the cut too large on the underside.

FIG 11

Console table

This project is fairly easy to undertake, but requires the ability to cut accurate 45-degree mitres for fitting the legs to the rails. These are best cut on a table-mounted circular saw or a chop saw, but a manual mitre saw will suffice as long as you mark the mitre all the way around the timber, clamp the wood to the saw bed and take it slowly.

After cutting, the legs are smoothed with a spokeshave; a rasp will do the job but takes a little longer. A template of the leg design is shown on page 253, but you should consider experimenting with alternative profiles. The only thing to remember is to minimize any short grain in the profile – this means any length of timber which has been cut diagonally across the grain, leaving an area, usually a point, which can snap off if the grain at the point is short in length. The danger points are at the tip or toe of the leg and, for want of a better term, the ankle, so don't be too flamboyant in your design.

To finish, the wood is stained using a solution of instant coffee and water, which gives an attractive aged look, and then rubbed with beeswax.

Essential Tools

pencil, tape, combination square, screwdriver, crosscut saw, jigsaw, spokeshave, electric drill, 3 mm wood bit, countersink bit, biscuit jointer and 10 size 20 biscuits, 12 mm bevel-edge chisel, jack plane, block plane, workbench, sash cramps and G-cramps

OTHER USEFUL TOOLS
table-mounted circular saw or chop saw, belt sander

Console table

Apart from the lipping around the edge of the table top, you can use ordinary deal timber, carefully selected for lack of knots.

You'll need to know

PREPARING WOOD
p. 16

BISCUIT JOINTER
p. 8

CUTTING MITRES
p. 21

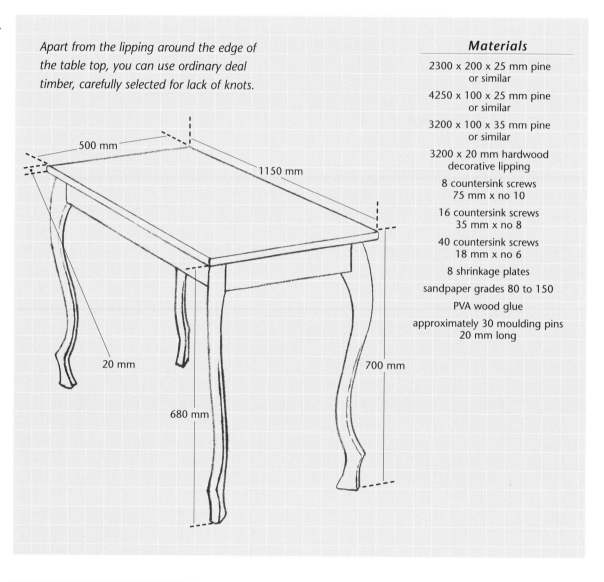

Materials

2300 x 200 x 25 mm pine
or similar

4250 x 100 x 25 mm pine
or similar

3200 x 100 x 35 mm pine
or similar

3200 x 20 mm hardwood
decorative lipping

8 countersink screws
75 mm x no 10

16 countersink screws
35 mm x no 8

40 countersink screws
18 mm x no 6

8 shrinkage plates

sandpaper grades 80 to 150

PVA wood glue

approximately 30 moulding pins
20 mm long

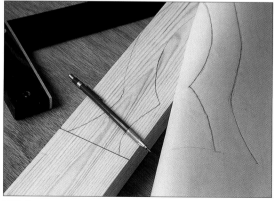

FIG 1

1 To start, you need to prepare the legs. Cut the 100 x 35 mm section timber into four equal lengths, and square each length across the ends. Measure up 680 mm and square another line around each leg. Take a tracing of the leg template on page 253, or make one of your own design, then lay it over one leg and press down the design through to the wood, reinforcing it with a pencil mark on the timber as you go (see Fig 1). Mark this leg as your pattern for shaping the other three.

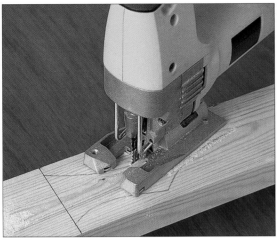

FIG 2

2 Ensure that the leg is secured to your work-bench, and carefully cut out to the line with a jigsaw (see Fig 2). Saw off the excess from the length with a hand saw or circular saw, and put aside. The offcuts from the legs will form the corner blocks that secure the legs of the table to the frame.

FIG 3

3 Shape the leg with a spokeshave, Surform tool or rasp (see Fig 3). When the cut is roughly square and you are happy with the basic shape, place it on the other three leg lengths, draw around it and repeat steps 2 and 3. Finish all the legs with a belt sander or sandpaper until they are smooth and even. Do not sand the tops of the legs at this stage.

TIP

To avoid damaging the faces of the rails when you tighten up the cramps, saw off the sharp points from the small scrap offcut blocks.

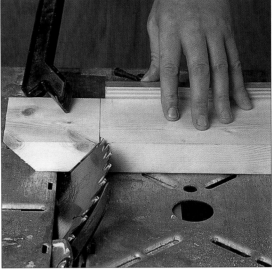

FIG 4

4 Fig 4 shows one of the offcut blocks being cut on a table saw, with the guard removed for the sake of clarity. The short point measurement (see step 5) is the same as the width of the back of the leg. Take care when cutting the blocks as it is essential that they are true and square; save the small offcuts.

5 To measure the rails from the 100 x 25 mm timber, take the "long points", the widest distance between two angled lines: looking down onto the wood edge, make two square lines across the edge at a given distance apart. Use the 45-degree shoulder of your combination square to make two further lines at 45 degrees running towards each other, from the same places as the two square lines. Cut two lengths mitred at 897 mm between the long points, and two at 347 mm.

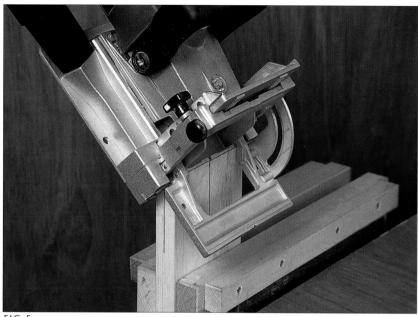

FIG 5

about one third into the mitre from the short point. Then draw a line along the mitred face and continue it onto the edges, so that you can align the registration marks on the footplate of the biscuit jointer. Clamp the rail in the vice as shown in Fig 5, set the jointer to the correct depth, then align the registration marks by adjusting the jointer's fence, and cut the slots for the biscuits (practise on some scrap beforehand). Then mark out the legs by transferring the marks from the rails onto the sides of the legs. The important thing to achieve in all this is that the short point of your rails should abut the back of the legs exactly. This is a tricky operation, so you will need to take care when you are marking out the legs.

6 Mark out the mitred ends of each rail by halving the width and carrying this mark over to the front and back faces. Then take a biscuit and find the optimum placing for the cut: it should be not too near the outside face, otherwise you will run the risk of the cutter splitting out – you should find that the best place is

7 Cut the 200 mm plank into two lengths, each of 1150 mm, and the remainder of the 100 x 25 mm plank to the same length. Place the best faces uppermost and arrange them as you think best, with the 100 mm between the 200 mm planks. To minimize any warping or bowing, place the end grain of each plank in alternate directions and mark these with a face mark. The centre line of the end biscuits should be about 50 mm from the ends of the planks, with all the other biscuits about 150 mm apart. Clamp each board face side uppermost to your bench, with a slight overhang along the edge. Set the jointer to cut along the centre of the edge, and align the registration mark with your pencil lines. Check that the depth is set to size 20 and cut all the slots on the three boards. Insert the biscuits as shown in Fig 6, then glue and clamp the boards.

FIG 6

FIG 7

8 When the top is completely dry, turn it over and plane off any irregularities. Now check that the ends are all flush; if not, cut them square with a circular or hand saw. Assemble the legs, rails and blocks, remembering to place the biscuits in the slots as you go. In Fig 7, you will see that small blocks have been used as packing for the clamp; these are the offcuts from the corner blocks. Drill out and countersink six holes for the screws. Drive the screws almost home, then check each corner for a square and tight fit. When you are satisfied that all the joints are good, disassemble the piece, glue up, clamp together and drive home the screws. Clean off any excess adhesive with a damp cloth and check the frame once more to ensure that it is absolutely true and square.

9 Place the edge lipping against the relevant edge and mark the short points. Cut the mitres with a tenon saw in a mitre block or in a mitre saw, and fix the edge lipping to the top, using glue and moulding pins. Clean up with a sharp chisel. When the assembly is completely dry, centre it over the upside-down table top and fix with the corner plates (see Fig 8). These have slots running in two directions, to allow movement of the top in relation to the rails. Place your screws in the middle of these slots, and use only the slot that runs parallel to the width of the top to fit the screws.

FIG 8

Birdhouse

This project is designed to be constructed with the minimum of tools and skills, although you can of course develop the basic idea. You will need to be aware of two things: first, the type of birds you wish to attract. The dimensions here are for the smaller tits; larger or more unusual birds will require different dimensions.

Second, you must make entry to the birdhouse by predators impossible. The chimney and bargeboards on the roof increase the weight, making it harder for the predator to dislodge, the extreme angle of the roof allows no footholds, and the epoxy glue coating around the entrance hole makes it difficult to enlarge the entrance hole by chewing to gain entrance.

There is one specialized tool used in this project. A gouge is a curved chisel, mainly used in the workshop for fitting curved mouldings to a mitre. It is used here to achieve a "Hansel and Gretel" look on the roof tiles, but you could just as easily use a normal chisel and have rectangular roof tiles.

Paint your birdhouse with ordinary emulsion, using a crackle glaze applied between two complementary shades, and finish with two coats of exterior varnish.

——— Essential Tools ———

pencil, tape, square, sliding bevel, Stanley knife, jigsaw with scrolling blade and straight cutting blade, electric drill, 6 and 25 mm wood bits, 19 mm gouge, jack plane, block plane, workbench, G-cramp

Birdhouse

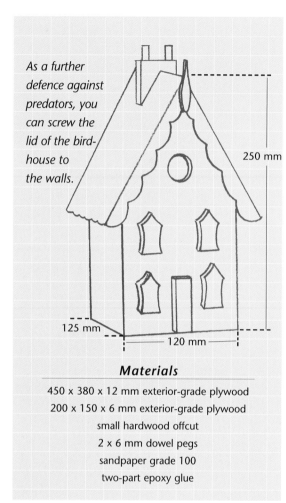

As a further defence against predators, you can screw the lid of the bird-house to the walls.

250 mm

125 mm

120 mm

Materials

450 x 380 x 12 mm exterior-grade plywood
200 x 150 x 6 mm exterior-grade plywood
small hardwood offcut
2 x 6 mm dowel pegs
sandpaper grade 100
two-part epoxy glue

Cutting list

all pieces cut from 12 mm plywood
2 pieces 220 x 120 mm (front and back)
2 pieces 100 x 110 mm (sides)
100 x 97 mm (base)
2 pieces 160 x 160 mm (roof)

FIG 2

2 To achieve the pitch of the roof, first mark a centre line through the front and back panels. Measure up from the base line of the front 110 mm to give the height of the side panels. Join the top of the centre line to the end of the 110 mm line; this gives the angle of the roof pitch. Set a sliding bevel to this angle and mark the angle on the back (see Fig 2). Cut out all the parts with a jigsaw or hand saw.

FIG 3

3 Place one of the sides of the roof in the jaws of your workbench and plane the angle of the ridge across the grain (see Fig 3), using your sliding bevel to check that the angle is true. Repeat for the matching piece.

FIG 1

1 Referring to the diagram and cutting list above, mark out a piece of 12 mm plywood (see Fig 1). In the photograph the thicker lines are the saw cuts, otherwise known as the kerf.

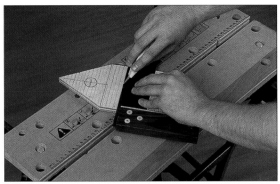

FIG 4

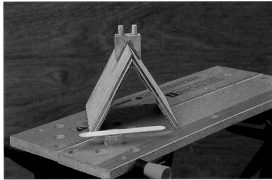

FIG 6

4 Mark a line across the faces every 8 mm or so; accuracy is not of paramount importance, but try to keep the lines square and parallel. Cut along each line with a craft knife held at an angle, as shown in Fig 4. Move along about a millimetre or so and make a further cut with the knife at the opposite angle to create a V-shape groove. When all the lines are cut, brush out the waste. Mark the entrance hole to 25 mm for small tits and 28 mm for slightly larger birds.

6 Position the chimney stack so that it acts as a simple clamp to hold the roof members together when you glue them up, as shown above in Fig 6.

FIG 7

7 Cut the fake door, windows, finial and bargeboards from the small offcut of 6 mm plywood, using a jigsaw (see Fig 7). Use some stylistic freedom here!

FIG 5

5 Mark out the roof tiles as shown in Fig 5. The lines are 25 mm apart, the width of a standard ruler, and the tiles are the width of the gouge. Each run is offset from its predecessor to resemble real roofing tiles. Cut the final line of tiles to its profile, using a jigsaw fitted with a scrolling blade. Drill the entrance hole using a flat bit or a hole saw. Measure and cut the chimney stack from some waste wood. Use the sliding bevel to determine the angle of the cutout, and drill two 6 mm holes in the top for the dowels.

FIG 8

8 Glue up the house as shown in Fig 8, using one clamp to hold the box. Liberally smear a layer of glue around the entrance hole, to strengthen it against predators. Attach the bargeboards and finial to the roof assembly.

Single wardrobe

This simple project, designed to be constructed with the absolute minimum of tools and skills, is based on construction techniques used by scenic carpenters in theatre, television and films. It uses triangular plywood plates and screws to replace the more usual jointing methods. This has two advantages: one, speed of construction, and the other, the materials can be easily recycled – so when you have tired of the wardrobe or your collection of designer suits has expanded beyond its capacity, you can unscrew it, remove the ply plates and adapt or expand it as required.

Seabird finials are called for here but you can, of course, indulge your own design talents. Just remember that whatever shape you design as a finial will be constrained by the 50 x 50 mm section of the corner posts. The sides and door are constructed from thick tongue-and-groove boards, to avoid warping and to provide sufficient thickness for the hinge. The finish is a thin emulsion wash with a dash of PVA added. Poster paints with PVA are used for the finials.

Essential Tools
---

pencil, tape, combination square, bradawl, screwdriver,
hammer, crosscut saw, coping saw, electric drill,
3 mm wood bit, countersink bit, workbench

OTHER USEFUL TOOLS
jigsaw with scrolling blade, belt sander

Single wardrobe

You'll need to know

FIXINGS & FITTINGS p. 14

PREPARING WOOD p. 16

SAWS pp. 6–10

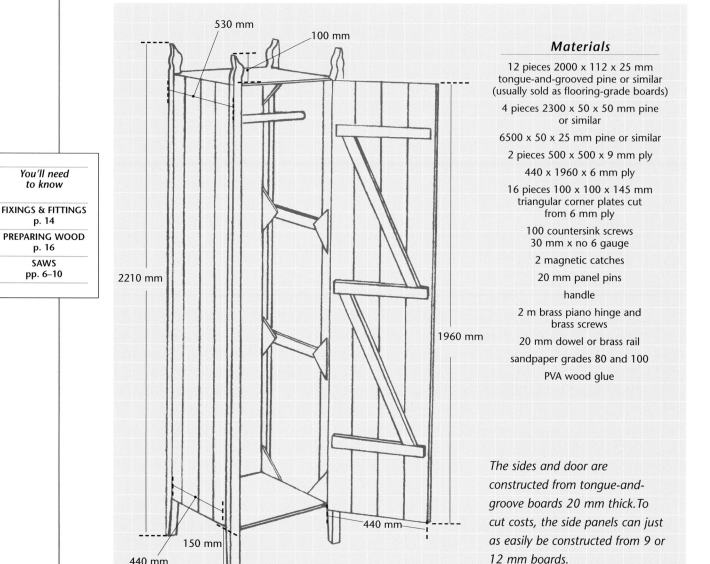

530 mm

100 mm

2210 mm

1960 mm

150 mm

440 mm

440 mm

Materials

12 pieces 2000 x 112 x 25 mm tongue-and-grooved pine or similar (usually sold as flooring-grade boards)

4 pieces 2300 x 50 x 50 mm pine or similar

6500 x 50 x 25 mm pine or similar

2 pieces 500 x 500 x 9 mm ply

440 x 1960 x 6 mm ply

16 pieces 100 x 100 x 145 mm triangular corner plates cut from 6 mm ply

100 countersink screws 30 mm x no 6 gauge

2 magnetic catches

20 mm panel pins

handle

2 m brass piano hinge and brass screws

20 mm dowel or brass rail

sandpaper grades 80 and 100

PVA wood glue

The sides and door are constructed from tongue-and-groove boards 20 mm thick. To cut costs, the side panels can just as easily be constructed from 9 or 12 mm boards.

1 To construct the sides, begin by cutting eight lengths of tongue-and-groove to 1960 mm. Select the best faces and position them in relation to each other, taking into account any warping or twist. Sort into two packs of four, slot together and plane or saw off the tongue from the end board. Cut eight 50 x 25 mm battens to the full width of the panels. Place two equidistant from the centre, and two 9 mm from the ends on each panel. Ensure that each batten lays square to the edges, and screw and glue them in place (see Fig 1). Stagger the screws and use two per board; if you are using thinner boards – for instance, 19, 12 or even 9 mm thickness – you will need shorter screws. Make sure, however, that you use 25 mm boards for the door.

FIG 1

2 For the door, repeat step 1, except for the three battens, which will be 50 mm shorter. Place one batten in the centre of the door, one 200 mm from the top and one 300 mm from the base. The top of the door will be determined by which side will take the hinge – this has to be the edge from which you have removed the tongue. Ensure the battens lay square to the door edge, and are placed 25 mm in from the edges. Screw and glue in place as in Fig 1.

3 To determine the length and angle required for the diagonals, place a length in position, look down from above and mark a line to cut to. Cut and screw and glue in place (see Fig 2). Cut the four corner posts to 2210 mm.

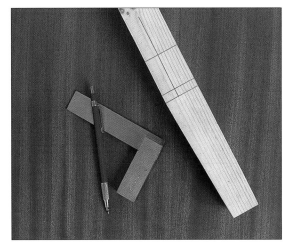

FIG 3

4 Mark the best two faces on each post, then mark each post as "front left", "rear left", etc. From the base measure up 150 mm, square round and mark a chamfer down to the base. The slope should run from the squared line taking 15 mm off the two best (outer) faces at the base of each post. Fig 3 shows a corner post with the chamfers cut. It is also marked out to show the position of the 9 mm floor of the wardrobe, the position of a side strut for the side panel and the amount of offset required when positioning the ply plates to allow the door to close. This offset will be the thickness of the door, plus 6 mm for the two front posts, but just 6 mm for the two rear posts to allow a flush fit for the 6 mm ply back.

FIG 2

FIG 4

FIG 6

5 Mark out the position of the 9 mm ply top on the corner posts, as shown by the two parallel lines in Fig 4. The distance from the upper mark to the bottom mark should be the height of the door, ie 1960 mm. To achieve a consistent profile for the finials, cut a template from a scrap of 6 mm plywood and draw your chosen design around it. Flip the template over for the left and right corner posts. Cut the profile with a coping or jigsaw, taking care to ensure that the cut is square to the front face and that the work is well supported.

7 To fit the side panels to the corner posts, select a pair of front and rear posts and arrange them parallel to each other with the outside faces down on the bench. Lay the side panel between the posts, ensuring that the panel is at the correct height in relation to the marks you made on the posts for the top and floor. At this point, the offset that you marked in step 3 becomes particularly important. Fig 6 shows a triangular plywood plate being screwed 6 mm in from the edge of the rear post using no 6 gauge countersink screws.

6 When you have finished cutting all four finials, wrap some sandpaper around a tube of silicone or something similar and use it to smooth out the saw cut marks, as shown in Fig 5. If you have the use of a belt sander, the front end or "nose" of the tool is quite perfectly suited for this smoothing job.

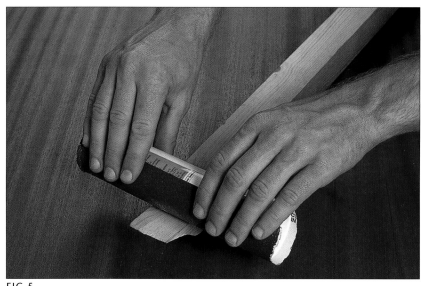

FIG 5

TIP

If you need to plane a bit from the door edge, remove the door, plane and then refit in place.

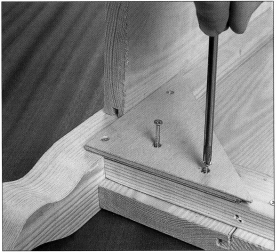

FIG 7

8 Use an offcut of the correct thickness to help position the plate (see Fig 7) – the thickness of the door (20 mm), plus 6 mm in from the edge of the front post. Pre-drill the plates as shown and allow the screws to pull up the side panel so that it lies flush with the upper face of the corner post.

9 The dimensions of the top and floor might vary, but essentially the width will be that of the door plus the thickness of two battens, plus 2 mm for fitting the hinge. The depth will be the width of a side panel plus the thickness of two corner posts, minus the two offsets. Fig 8 shows the ply floor fitted to one side.

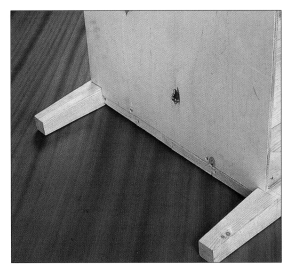

FIG 9

10 Cut and true the ply to size, then cut notches at each corner to accommodate the posts. To fit the top and floor, lay one side face-down and screw the ply in place. Rotate the entire assembly through 90 degrees onto the front face and fit the other side. To fit the back, put small offcut blocks between the ply plates at the back and set them in by 6 mm, the same as the rear plates. Check the carcass is square, cut a 6 mm ply panel to fit and fix with glue and pins. Rotate the carcass again so that the hinge side is face down. Fit the door, supporting the outer edge with a small block. Fit the hinge with screws every 400 mm.

FIG 8

Screen

A screen is normally thought of as three or four panels connected by hinges. However, you can use as many panels as you wish – 24 panels are used here, and are connected with rope. A router table, a useful addition to the home workshop that turns your router into a small spindle moulder, will speed up the tedious part of this project and should ensure greater accuracy in the fit of the male and female profiles.

You can use almost any timber – a maple or sycamore screen with stainless-steel cleats would look very stylish, if somewhat extravagant. When selecting the timber at a yard, be firm in refusing any length that is twisted or warped, or has dry knots on either edge.

For the finish, an interior colour wash blended with a small amount of gold powder is used. The tassels used to hide the ends of the nylon ropes have a wooden flange on the top, through which the nylon is threaded and is then tied off under the body of the tassel.

Essential Tools

pencil, tape, square, screwdriver, tenon saw, jigsaw, electric drill, 6 mm extra-long multi-speed bit, 6 and 7 mm twist bits, 12 mm flat bit, block plane, large sash cramp or cramp heads, router mounted on router table, half-round cutter 6 mm radius, ogee cutter 6 mm radius, workbench

Screen

**You'll need
to know**

ROUTER TABLE
p. 8
PREPARING WOOD
p. 16
ROUTING
pp. 19–21

Although this project uses modern nylon rope and cleats, and the joining profiles have been adapted for use with a standard router cutter or spindle moulder, it is essentially the same design that has been used for hundreds of years in the Far East. Older screens of this type would have been made of what was then a plentiful supply of hard-wood, but pine or a similar softwood will do just as well.

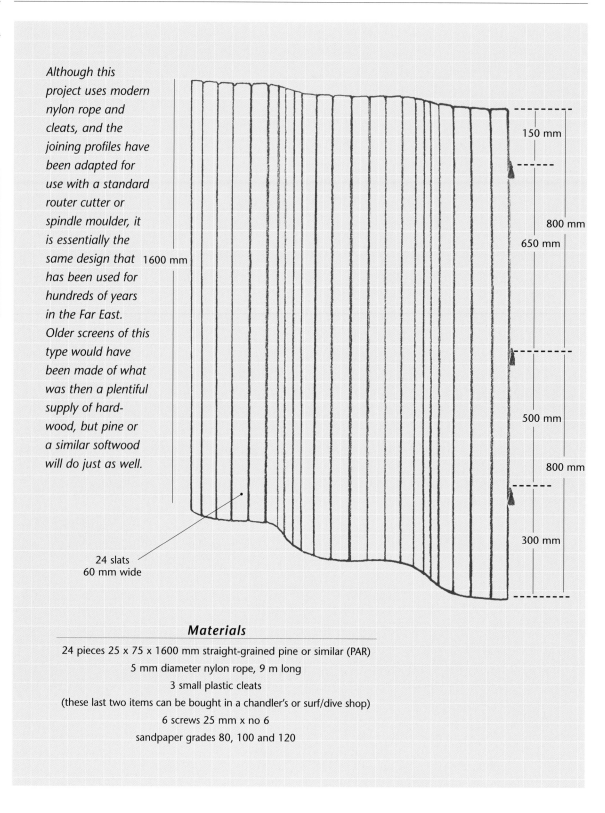

1600 mm

150 mm

800 mm

650 mm

500 mm

800 mm

300 mm

24 slats
60 mm wide

Materials

24 pieces 25 x 75 x 1600 mm straight-grained pine or similar (PAR)

5 mm diameter nylon rope, 9 m long

3 small plastic cleats

(these last two items can be bought in a chandler's or surf/dive shop)

6 screws 25 mm x no 6

sandpaper grades 80, 100 and 120

FIG 1

FIG 2

1 Cut 24 lengths of timber to 1.6 m long. Mark each length with a corresponding number (from 1 to 24) and mark a top. Number 1 will be the left-hand-side plank; make a mark on the edge halfway down, i.e. at 800 mm. Make a further mark 150 mm from the top, and another 300 mm from the base, ensuring that these marks are in the centre of the edge. Use a square to transfer these marks to the other edge. Clamp all the planks together, edge uppermost, and transfer the marks from plank 1 to all the others. Turn the pack over and repeat. Secure plank 1 in your vice and drill three 12 mm holes 12 mm deep to conceal the initial knots of the ropes, as shown in Fig 1.

TIP

If you are in any doubt whatsoever as to your competence in fusing the rope as demonstrated in step 7, you can get a good result by taping the ends with electrical tape.

---

2 Use a 6 mm extra-long bit to drill the holes through which the rope will pass in plank 1 (see Fig 2). Drill halfway through, keeping the bit square to the timber at all times, then drill from the other edge. If you find a slight misalignment, correct this with a small round file. A pillar drill or drill stand will speed up this process. Drill three 6 mm holes in the remaining planks.

3 Fit a 6 mm radius ovolo cutter to your router, then mount the router in the router table. Use a scrap piece to set the fence in position. Depending on the type of table you are using, the fence, in all probability, will be set at a slight angle across the centre of the cutter. The height of the cut should be to the centre line of the timber's edge, and the thickness should be so you just skim the centre edge with the cutter. The uppermost part of the profile should just touch the centre line drawn across the edge of each plank.

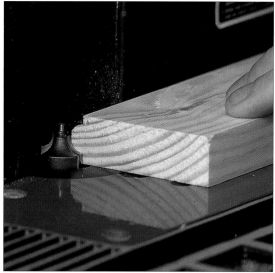

FIG 3

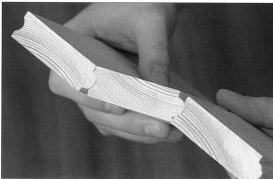

FIG 5

6 Fig 5 shows in detail how the two profiles should match. Pass the left-hand side of all planks, except plank 1, through the router. Lay all the planks in order on the workbench.

4 To achieve the profile, you need to make two passes, turning the timber over after the first cut (see Fig 3). When you are sure that the profile is correct, cut the edge of plank 1 that does not have the 12 mm holes drilled; this should be to the right-hand side of the plank. Then cut all the other planks on the right-hand side, except plank 24, which should be left square on the right-hand side.

7 Cut the rope into three equal lengths. Nylon rope will fray at the ends unless taped or fused. The best method is to fuse the ends together with the flame from a cigarette lighter. Make a clean cut while the rope is held taut. Take the new end and twist the rope in the direction that it falls. Run the flame of a cigarette lighter under the rope about 50 mm away from the end you are holding. Rotate the rope round and move the lighter over a 20 mm section. As soon as you can see the outer surface fusing together, remove the flame and cool the rope in water.

5 To shape the tops, use a coin about 20 mm in diameter and place it so that it touches the top edge and the reveal of the ovolo cut. Draw around it. Place the coin against the edge and the top on the other edge, and mark. Using a jigsaw, cut square through the ovolo profile to the lines. Change the cutter in the router to a half-round with a 6 mm radius. Again, use a test piece to position the fence and the height of the cutter, then make the cut (see Fig 4).

FIG 4

FIG 6

FIG 7

8 Make a new cut in the middle of the section you have fused together. This process needs to be done at both ends of all three ropes. Tie a figure-of-eight knot at one end (see Fig 6), to act as a stopper in the 12 mm holes in plank 1.

9 Starting from plank 1, thread each rope through one plank at a time (see Fig 7). Twist the rope with the lay, and if you find a hole tight, ream it out with a 6 mm drill bit. Push each plank up tight as you work.

TIP

When routing the planks, take it slowly and keep a firm pressure downwards. You may find it easier to enlist the help of an assistant to draw the planks from you as they come off the table.

FIG 8

10 Use a large sash cramp to pull the planks together. Screw a plastic cleat just under each hole, pulling the ropes as tight as you can, and lock them off in the cleats (see Fig 8). Offer up the tassels, if used; cut and fuse the ropes to the shortest possible length, then place the tassels in position, fixing them with glue or cotton binding.

Waney shelves

"Waney" or "waney edge" refers to timber with the bark attached to one or more faces. Fine walnut is used here, but you could also make similar shelving using long, straight planks with a waney surface on the front edge.

Cutting and finishing the shelves is not difficult; the cunning bit is the hidden wall fixing. Here, 10 mm diameter stainless steel rods are inserted in the back edge, and then car body filler is fixed into both the shelf and the wall. If fitting into a corner, a nylon connecting block can be recessed into the edge to provide additional support. This method is fairly straightforward if you are fixing to a brick or stone wall, but if you live in a timber-framed house or you want to hang these shelves from a stud partition wall, a different approach must be taken.

Remove the plaster or dry wall lining from the fixing areas, from the other side of the wall. Drill through the exposed timber uprights with a 10 mm drill, insert 10 mm threaded rods, fix the rods into the shelf with body filler and when dry, tighten up the nuts from the other side and cut the rods flush to the nut's surface. Plaster over the holes and make good.

--- Essential Tools ---

pencil, straightedge, tape, square, spirit level,
half-round file, electric drill, 10 mm wood bit, 9 mm
masonry bit, jigsaw, jack plane, block plane,
cabinet scraper, workbench

OTHER USEFUL TOOLS
router with straight cutter (if fitting connecting block
side support)

Waney shelves

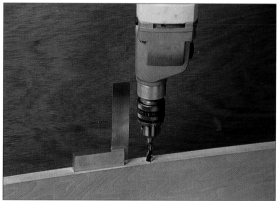

Check the angle at which your walls meet first – they may not be at right angles.

Third cut

Second cut

First cut

Materials

Hardwood with an interesting grain and at least one waney edge. It will need to be purchased with a specific site in mind, and this will determine the length and width, but the finished thickness should be about 25 to 35 mm

10 mm diameter stainless steel rod, about 200 mm for every fixing point

Two-part "elastic" car body filler

Sandpaper grades 60 to 240

You'll need to know

PREPARING WOOD
p. 16

ROUTING
pp. 19–21

1 Select the board, assess the most advantageous shape to cut and mark it out very carefully. This triangular piece had a waney edge on both edges, with a sawn edge to the right-hand side. If the shelves are to be part of a set when they are fixed, consider the overall shape, the direction and the colouring of the grain and, most importantly, the curves and the edge bevels.

FIG 1

2 Slice off the bulk of the bark with a chisel, and use a belt sander with a coarse belt to rapidly remove all the remaining fibrous matter, or phloem (see Fig 1). You can use the nose of the tool to follow the undulations of the timber. Plane the straight edges and the two faces and finish them with a cabinet scraper as normal.

FIG 2

3 Drill 10 mm diameter holes along the back edge of each shelf – around 300–400 mm between each centre should be sufficient. The rods need to go into the shelf at least 100 mm deep. Use a square to assist you in keeping your drill perpendicular (see Fig 2), and if your shelf is tapered, be careful to avoid breakout on the front edge where the shelf narrows.

TIP

To ensure that the shelves will fit when cut, make a small card model at 1:10 or 1:12 scale beforehand.

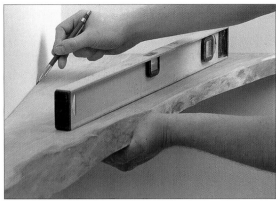

FIG 3

4 Scribe the shelves to get an exact fit up to the wall. This is particularly important if you decide to use a support method as outlined on page 189. The greater the area of contact with the wall, the better your fixing will be. Use a spirit level when marking the wall, and then use this line to scribe to (see Fig 3). At the same time, mark a further line on the wall for the underside of the shelf.

FIG 4

5 Each steel rod should be 10 mm shorter than the hole drilled into the back edge of your shelves, plus a minimum of 100 mm into the wall. The deeper you can fix into the wall, the better, as the shelf will be stronger. Attach your drill to a bench vice, insert the rods and use a file as shown to round off each end slightly (see Fig 4). Also cut a "key" along the length of each rod. This will assist the filler in bonding with the stainless steel.

FIG 5

6 If you are fitting the shelves in an alcove or a corner, a way to achieve even greater hidden support is to rout out a channel in the side edge of each shelf. This should be of sufficient width and depth to receive half a nylon connector block. Start the channel about 80 mm from the back of the shelf, and stop it just short of the front (see Fig 5).

7 Insert the rods into the back edge and carefully mark the wall between the upper and lower lines. Drill out the wall using an undersized bit, in this case 9 mm for a brick wall; concrete or stone will require a full-sized 10 mm bit.

FIG 6

8 Mark for the connector block, if used. It needs to be sited the length of the protruding rods, plus 10 mm forward from the back wall. The rods can then be inserted into the wall, and when the shelf is pushed back into place, the nylon block will slide along its channel until the shelf is fully in place (see Fig 6). Hammer home the rods. Coat the wall, the protruding rods and the back edge and holes of the shelf with filler and push the shelf home. Do a dry run, and only apply the filler when you are sure all fits. Clean off any excess filler with a sharp knife before it has set fully.

Kitchen accessories

Here are two projects that utilize offcuts – which you should never discard. In both, the dimensions are to some degree flexible, depending on what you have to hand.

The chopping board is designed to be a mini version of a butcher's block, with end grain uppermost. Every block within the outer frame is a regular cross section cut from various odd lengths. If you wish to follow the herringbone arrangement illustrated, this regularity is essential. However, you can create a pattern of random widths all glued up together. The frame is dovetailed together using a single pin with an angle of 1:8. This is a simple joint, but requires a fair degree of accuracy and concentration. For the knife rack (shown on page 196), two contrasting timbers are separated by 6 mm plywood fillets. The chopping board is finished with olive oil (you could use any vegetable oil), and the knife rack with Danish oil.

Essential Tools

pencil, tape, square, sliding bevel, tenon saw or dovetail saw, crosscut saw, bevel-edge chisel, coping saw, jigsaw, electric drill, 4 mm wood bit, countersink bit, jack plane, block plane, cabinet scraper, Flexicurve or French curves, workbench, G-cramps

OTHER USEFUL TOOLS
table-mounted circular saw, belt sander, electric hand plane

Chopping board

285 mm

355 mm

45 mm

30 mm

Materials

2 pieces 360 x 45 x 30 mm maple
2 pieces 300 x 45 x 30 mm maple
95 pieces 47 x 45 x 20 mm ash
two-part epoxy resin

**You'll need
to know**

PREPARING WOOD
p. 16

SAWS
pp. 6–10

FIG 1

1 Collect together short lengths of timber of the same section, about 45 x 20 mm; you will need about 4.5–5 m in total. Saw these accurately to 47 mm, ensuring that there are no defects near either end (see Fig 1). Arrange them in rows of 12 in a herringbone pattern to create the main block. Cut two lengths of softwood batten 150 mm longer than the length of your assembled block and two lengths about 10 mm less than the width of the block.

FIG 2

2 Arrange the blocks, battens and cramps as shown in Fig. 2, then lay a sheet of newspaper over your bench and quickly apply some epoxy glue to all four faces of each block. Place the battens and clamps in place and tighten. If any outer block tends to pull away from the main body, adjust the position or tightness of the nearest cramp head, or force a small wedge of timber into the side of the batten to correct the error. Scrape off any excess glue and clean up. When the glue has dried, plane one face flat and mark a square area, using the maximum amount of the block (see Fig 7 on page 196); it may be a good idea to allow a 2 mm margin of error in from the extreme edge of the block as it's far easier to plane the edge of the block than have to re-cut dovetail shoulders. This marked area will be the inside dimension of your frame. Prepare the frame parts and transfer the marks from the block to give the shoulders of the dovetails.

3 Mark out for the dovetails: square the shoulder marks round, then square round a second line the thickness of the timbers (30 mm) out from the shoulder line. You will have some excess length, called "horns". Set a sliding bevel to a 1:8 slope – measure a line 80 mm long on scrap wood, then mark a second line running square to the first 10 mm long and join the two lines with a diagonal to give a 1 in 8 bevel. For the pins, set a marking gauge to 10 mm and mark a point in from the edge on the second line drawn. Repeat at both ends, front and back, and on both short lengths.

FIG 3

FIG 4

4 Use the sliding bevel with the stock against the narrow face to draw a line intersecting the 10 mm point down to the shoulder line. Repeat back and front and both ends. Join the bevels across the end grain and mount the timber vertically in a vice. Saw just to the outside of your bevel lines, keeping the saw level. As you approach the shoulder line, check the back to ensure that you don't cut too deep. Turn the work to a horizontal position and cut to the shoulder line, just leaving the line in place (see Fig 3).

5 Mark out the sockets in the same fashion on the longer lengths: the stock of the sliding bevel will lie against the narrow edge as before, but this time the blade runs across the end grain. Use the marking gauge at 10 mm to run from the end grain down to the shoulder line, and reset it to the thickness of the narrowest width of the peg, about 17 mm. Run this line down to the shoulder. Prior to cutting the sockets, lay all four lengths out on the bench and check that you have marked them correctly.

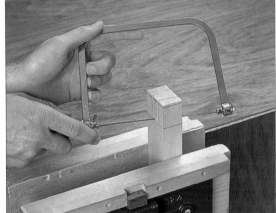

FIG 5

6 Mount the work vertically in the vice or workbench jaws and saw down to the shoulder lines as shown in Fig 4.

7 Remove the waste with a coping saw, as shown in Fig 5, taking care not to go too close to the shoulder line. Whatever you leave will have to be removed with a chisel later. Check the back shoulder line repeatedly as you saw.

8 Use a sharp bevel-edge chisel to remove the remaining waste. Only chisel to just past the middle of the socket, then turn the work around and come in from the other side. Keep the tool level, and don't attempt to remove too much in one go. If you encounter any resistance, give a light tap with a mallet – don't use the palm of your hand!

TIP

Coping saws are difficult to control, owing to the narrowness of the blade, so check the cut continuously.

195

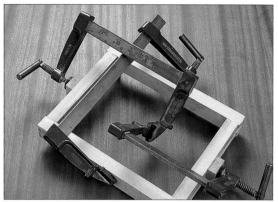

FIG 6

9 When all the joints have been cut, try a dry run. You may need to pare a small amount from the pins or the shoulders; if so, take the wood off with a chisel, a shaving at a time. When fitting the joints, do not force them in any way or you run the risk of splitting the sockets. When you have a perfect fit, lay the work on a flat surface and prepare to glue up (see Fig 6). If your cramps are too short, use two in line. When dry, saw off the horns; take care not to mark the surface.

FIG 7

10 Scrape any glue residue from the inside of the frame and lay it over the main block. Check for fit, then saw the waste from the block, using a jigsaw, hand saw or circular saw (see Fig 7). Adjust if necessary by planing the edge and the back face of the block, using a belt sander fitted with a flat sanding plate and finishing with a block plane. Glue the block inside the frame, using a liberal coating of glue. When dry, use a block plane on the end grain of the dovetails. Plane off a 2 mm arris from all sharp edges.

Knife rack

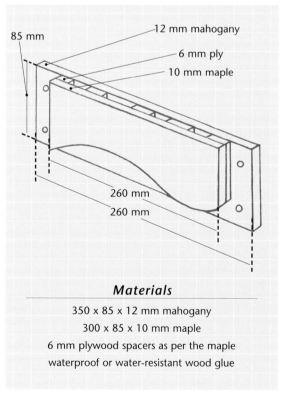

85 mm

12 mm mahogany

6 mm ply

10 mm maple

260 mm

260 mm

Materials

350 x 85 x 12 mm mahogany

300 x 85 x 10 mm maple

6 mm plywood spacers as per the maple

waterproof or water-resistant wood glue

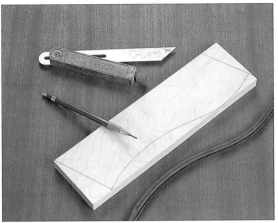

FIG 8

11 Prepare the maple front and mahogany back as per the cutting list. Mark up by setting the bevel to 20 degrees and laying the stock across the end. Draw a curve freehand or by using a Flexicurve (see Fig 8) or French curves, then cut with a jigsaw fitted with a fine blade. Use the maple as a template to copy the shape onto the plywood, and cut it out. The mahogany back needs a bevel at each end only.

FIG 10

13 Lay the plywood over the back, spacing the knives as you go, as shown in Fig 10. Mark the outlines with a pencil. Using waterproof wood adhesive according to the manufacturer's instructions, glue up the workpiece as a sandwich. Clamp up using one centrally placed large G-cramp or two equally spaced smaller ones, checking continually that none of the plywood spacers has slipped.

FIG 9

12 Lay the plywood on the back and position all the knives that you intend to use in position. Use a sharp pencil to draw around them accurately, leaving a gap of approximately 0.5 mm from the blade (as shown in Fig 9). Make sure that you identify the waste wood by crosshatching to avoid confusion, and then cut the plywood into strips.

FIG 11

14 Leave the assembly to dry, preferably overnight. When it is completely dry, mark out four equally spaced 3 mm screw holes, using a ruler as a guide for spacing, as shown in Fig 11. Drill the holes, using a countersink bit, and tidy the edges up if necessary. Finally drill wall holes, insert wall plugs and screw the rack to the wall at a 20-degree angle.

Stacking storage units

A simple method of securely jointing the thin boards used in this project is to use finger joints. These are castellations running along the end of one board, with a similar set cut into the adjacent board. For the better equipped workshop, especially if you see yourself wanting to make any quantity of lightweight plywood furniture or storage boxes, invest in a template cutter; this project uses a finger joint template. With a template such as this it is possible to cut two boards of up to 300 mm wide at once, ranged side by side; however, for the sake of clarity it is shown here being used just on one side. When you have mastered this simple jointing technique the possibilities are endless, enabling you to make a wide range of modern furniture simply, quickly and perhaps profitably!

The internal dimensions will be governed by what you intend to store: the antiqued baskets shown opposite can be obtained in a wide range of sizes. But a further consideration could well be the dimensions of your stereo or video, etc. Just draw out the external dimensions of the items, add 5 mm on each side, top and bottom, and twice the thickness of the ply to obtain the outside dimensions of the unit.

Essential Tools

pencil, steel rule or tape, square, marking knife, circular saw, router with 8 mm and 9.5 mm straight cutters, dovetail cutting jig with finger-jointing plate to suit your router, 6 mm and 9 mm bevel-edge chisels, jack plane, block plane, sash cramps, workbench

Stacking storage units

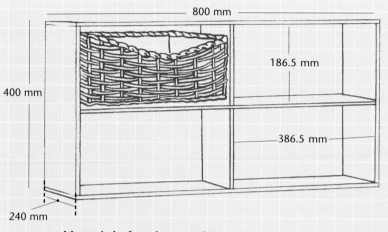

800 mm

400 mm

186.5 mm

386.5 mm

240 mm

When working with plywood, it is essential to guard against splitting or breaking out of the surface. Before each cut or router pass, score the top surface with a craft or marking knife.

You'll need to know

PREPARING WOOD
p. 16

ROUTING
pp. 19–21

Materials for three units

2440 x 1220 x 9.5 mm birch-faced plywood (boxes)
1220 x 800 x 6 mm MDF or plywood (backs)
PVA wood glue
20 mm moulding pins
sandpaper grades 100 and 150

Cutting list per unit

2 pieces 800 x 240 x 9.5 mm (top and base)
2 pieces 400 x 240 x 9.5 mm (sides)
790 x 234 x 9.5 mm (middle shelf)
2 pieces 234 x 194.5 x 9.5 mm (shelf dividers)
791 x 391 x 6 mm (back)

FIG 1

1 The most economical method of cutting a sheet of ply to the cutting list is to cut the top, sides and the middle shelf all running across the board, with the shelf dividers then taken from the waste. Mark and cut each component one by one. Before cutting, use a sharp knife to score the face of the board with two parallel lines the width of the kerf. Clamp a straight length of timber securely to the board as a guide fence for the saw, as shown in Fig 1.

FIG 2

2 Sort the sides, bottoms and tops of the unit into groups. On the inside faces of each piece, mark the shoulders of the finger joints using the adjacent component as a guide (see Fig 2). Repeat this process for all the joints.

FIG 3

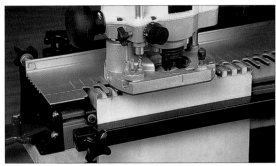

FIG 5

3 Fit the finger-jointing template in place of the normal dovetail one, inserting a block of MDF (medium-density fibreboard) to prevent your work splitting (see Fig 3). It must be square and true on the front edge and placed in line with the cut line on the template surface. The smaller piece of MDF in the foreground will keep the template flat.

4 Clamp the template to the bench with a slight overhang at the front. Fit the 11 mm guide plate (supplied with the template) and an 8 mm straight cutter to your router. Mount the work, ensuring that the upper surface is perfectly aligned with the top of the anti-breakout block and that the work is clamped securely. Use the fine adjuster on the router to lower the cutter exactly to the pencil line drawn in step 2. Rout out all the top and base parts at both ends, working left to right.

FIG 4

5 The template comes supplied with two 8 mm stop pins. These shift the work over 8 mm, thereby allowing the pins and sockets of the finger joints to line up. Insert the stop pins with a screwdriver (see Fig 4), then fit and cut the side panels as for the top and bottom.

6 Sort the sides, tops and bottoms into separate sets and plane the front and rear edges clean. Use the 8 mm straight cutter in your router and fit a fence set to cut a rebate 6 mm wide on the rear edge, inside face for the back (see Fig 5). The rebate should be 5 mm deep and must stop just short of the pencil lines marked in step 2. Use a 6 mm chisel to square the ends of the rebate to the line.

FIG 6

7 Ascertain the centre of the middle shelf, the top and the bottom shelves. Scribe two lines 9 mm apart with a knife and, using a fence as shown in Fig 6, rout out the rebate to take the vertical shelf dividers. The depth of cut for the top and bottom is 5 mm. For the middle shelf, cut only to 3 mm on either side. Clean up the rebates with a chisel. Assemble flat on the bench, check for fit and square, adjust as required, then glue up. For speedy finishing, the use of a belt sander is recommended. Check the internal measurements for the back, cut 6 mm plywood to fit and fix in place with moulding pins.

Corner cabinet

This corner cupboard with pierced doors is an exercise in cutting simple joints. It uses what is probably the most basic joint of all, the corner halving, made by cutting halfway through the thickness of the timber with a tenon saw and then removing the waste with a chisel. The outer surface of the wood is left just a little rough, giving the piece a rustic, cottagey feel.

The beading along the top is called "egg and dart". To fit this type of beading correctly will entail some complicated setting-out, so you may wish to replace this with a plain bead of similar size. The piercing can also be simplified. If you wish the piercing to be symmetrical and have both a left and right hand, use a MDF (medium-density fibreboard) template as a stencil to transfer the design to your doors and flip the template to get both the left and right hand sides.

This cupboard is painted with a coat of rust emulsion then overpainted with jade, which is rubbed with fine wire wool to reveal a hint of the underlying colour. The brass handles and hinges are complemented by the gold paint on the inner faces of the piercing.

─────── Essential Tools ───────

pencil, tape, combination square, sliding bevel,
screwdriver, hammer, mallet, crosscut saw, tenon saw,
jigsaw with scroll blade, electric drill, 3 mm, 4 mm and
8 mm wood bits, countersink bit, 25 mm bevel-edge
chisel, jack plane, block plane,
workbench, G-cramps

OTHER USEFUL TOOLS
table-mounted circular saw, belt sander, electric planer

Corner cabinet

You'll need
to know

PREPARING WOOD
p. 16

SAWS
pp. 6–10

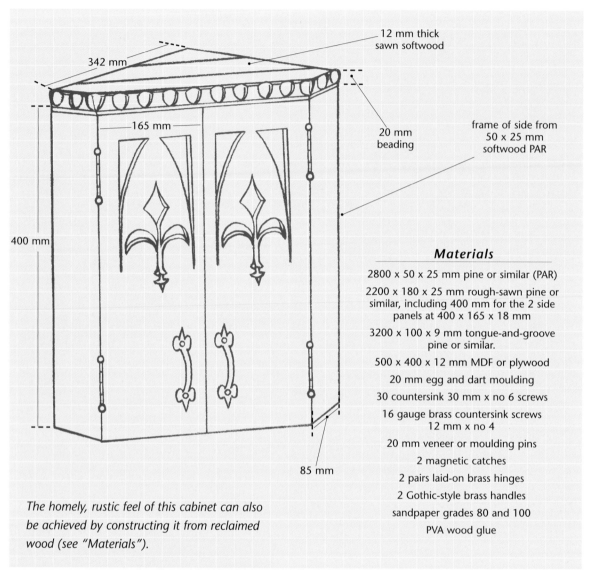

12 mm thick
sawn softwood

342 mm

165 mm

400 mm

20 mm
beading

frame of side from
50 x 25 mm
softwood PAR

85 mm

*The homely, rustic feel of this cabinet can also
be achieved by constructing it from reclaimed
wood (see "Materials").*

Materials

2800 x 50 x 25 mm pine or similar (PAR)

2200 x 180 x 25 mm rough-sawn pine or
similar, including 400 mm for the 2 side
panels at 400 x 165 x 18 mm

3200 x 100 x 9 mm tongue-and-groove
pine or similar.

500 x 400 x 12 mm MDF or plywood

20 mm egg and dart moulding

30 countersink 30 mm x no 6 screws

16 gauge brass countersink screws
12 mm x no 4

20 mm veneer or moulding pins

2 magnetic catches

2 pairs laid-on brass hinges

2 Gothic-style brass handles

sandpaper grades 80 and 100

PVA wood glue

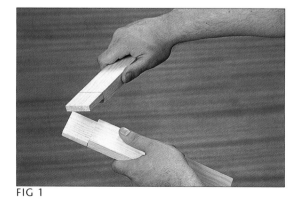

FIG 1

1 Make two frames from 50 x 25 mm sections of deal, with the outside dimensions of one frame 280 x 400 mm, and 300 x 400 mm for the other. Cut four lengths at 400 mm, two at 280 mm and two at 300 mm, and mark the width of the timber on the faces at the ends of all lengths and half the width, using a marking gauge. Cut the corner halving joints as shown in Fig 1. Glue up and clamp each frame, ensuring that they are square.

FIG 2

2 Join the two frames together, using the edge of your workbench to ensure that they are square (see Fig 2). The wider frame overlaps the other, giving an equal length. Glue and screw using three 30 mm screws.

FIG 3

FIG 4

3 Prepare the sawn timber. You need two doors at 400 x 165 x 18 mm, two side panels at 400 x 85 x 20 mm, one top at 170 x 330 x 12 mm and the other top at 130 x 490 x 12 mm. The idea is to keep some of the rough quality of the timber, but not so much as to give you splinters; a belt sander run along the face is the best method, as shown in Fig 3. To plane down the rear face of the timbers, use an electric plane – don't plane the front faces!

4 Plane a 45-degree bevel on the inner edges of the side panels; this bevel is fixed to the hinges. Measuring from the back of each panel, the bevel needs to be in excess of the thickness of the doors: 22 mm is a good dimension, and will leave a small flat as shown in Fig 4. The hinge pin sits up to this flat. Screw the sides to the frames, recessing the screws a little. If you wish, you can fill in these screw holes prior to painting the cabinet.

FIG 5

FIG 6

5 Sit the assembly over the MDF to form the base of the cupboard. Draw around the inside of the frame (see Fig 5). When you draw inside the side bevels, take your line up to the small flat at the front of the bevel on each side and join these two points with a straight edge. Check the base for square and ensure both sides are equal, as this base will govern the finished shape of the cupboard. Cut out the shape you have drawn and finish off with a plane. Place the side and frame assembly up to the MDF and check the fit. Butt up the doors from the small flat on the side panels, sitting them on the MDF.

6 Reach inside the cupboard and mark the position of each door at the hinge edge. Join the marks with a straightedge. Make sure you are accurate, otherwise the doors will not meet correctly when closed. Cut to the line, plane true and then screw the frame assembly to the MDF. Line the inside of the frames with the tongue-and-groove lengths; start at one corner and work forward, nailing each length once the entire side has been fitted (see Fig 6). The final length on each side will need to be cut along its length to suit.

FIG 7

7 Take the two parts for the top, the wider being to the rear of the top. Place it on the cupboard and mark the 45-degree angles from the underside. Cut and screw down to the frame. The front part of the top is a little more complicated, as it needs to be cut as a lozenge shape, as shown in Fig 7. It butts up to the other part of the top and is flush to the frame at the back, but has an overhang of 20 mm at the sides and the front. The join of the beading should be at a proper place in the design, allowing the pattern of the beading to continue uninterrupted as the mitres are made.

8 Take a length of beading and cut a 67.5 degree mitre with the front of the cut in the centre of one of the darts. Hold this length up to the front of the top and choose a further dart centre at the far end. Cut back at 67.5 degrees from this new point. The short points at the rear of the beading will determine the length of the front of the top, hence the overhang, which you should duplicate for the overhang of the sides.

FIG 8

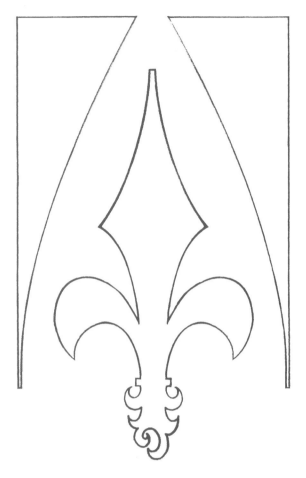

This template for the cutout on the doors is shown here slightly over half-size. Make sure that any variations match the dimensions of the doors.

9 Fit the beading to the top with moulding pins, leaving an upstand to form a false cornice (see Fig 8). Fit the hinges to the sides at regular spacing, try the doors in place, and adjust as required by planing. There should be a gap all around the doors of about 1 mm.

10 When the doors fit, cut a template from some MDF (above right). Cut out the template with a jigsaw, ensuring the edges are square and smooth (Fig 9). Place the template over the door and spray on some paint, making sure that you get into all the corners. Flip the template and spray the other door. Cut both doors with a jigsaw. Sand off excess paint. Hang the doors, fit the handles and catches. Fill all screw holes with filler, and paint.

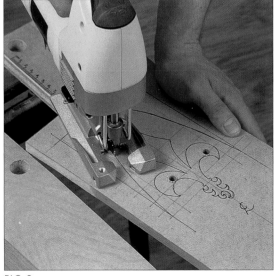

FIG 9

Picture rail shelf

This simple shelving system can be fixed to the walls of a room by wall plugs and screws, giving you a fashionable display and storage space that is quick and easy to construct. The height will vary according to the ceiling height of your room, but about 300 mm above head height would be normal. It may also be fixed at dado rail height, about 800 mm from the floor.

Normally, the shelf would be fixed around all the walls, with breaks for any windows or doors. When measuring the length you'll need to take into account any external mitres that need to be cut; in a modern house the rooms are usually rectangular, with no external mitres required, but in older houses you may have a chimney breast protruding into the room, which will require a mitre on either side. All the internal angles are simple butt joints. The pegs are fixed at 300 mm centres here, but they can be at any regular spacing. Note that the pegs are slightly angled upwards, at 80 degrees to the face of the support, to stop things falling off them.

The timber is softwood that is primed and undercoated prior to fixing, and is finished with eggshell paint when in place.

─────────── Essential Tools ───────────

pencil, tape, combination square, sliding bevel,
screwdriver, mitre saw, electric drill, 25 mm hole saw
or flat bit, 4 mm wood bit, countersink bit, 25 mm
bevel-edge chisel, mallet, block plane, workbench,
spirit level

Picture rail shelf

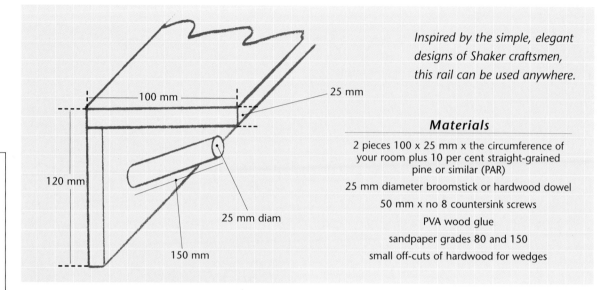

Inspired by the simple, elegant designs of Shaker craftsmen, this rail can be used anywhere.

Materials

2 pieces 100 x 25 mm x the circumference of your room plus 10 per cent straight-grained pine or similar (PAR)

25 mm diameter broomstick or hardwood dowel

50 mm x no 8 countersink screws

PVA wood glue

sandpaper grades 80 and 150

small off-cuts of hardwood for wedges

You'll need to know

DRILL BITS
p. 11

PLANING
p. 18

CUTTING MITRES
p. 21

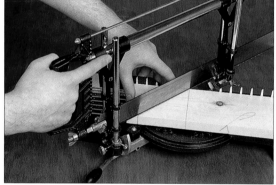

FIG 1

1 Cut the 100 x 25 mm timber into two lengths, one for the shelf and one for the support. When calculating the lengths, start in one corner of the room and work your way around. The first support will be the full extent of the wall, but subsequent ones will be shorter by the thickness of the preceding one; the shelf measurement will also reduce by the width of the preceding one. The easiest method of cutting a mitre is to mark the actual length of the wall on the shelf, taking into account any reduction, then square across the timber and mark the mitre along the face using a combination square. Cut using a mitre saw (Fig 1) or a mitre block and tenon saw.

2 Transfer the measurement, allowing for the different reduction, to the matching support part and cut as demonstrated before.

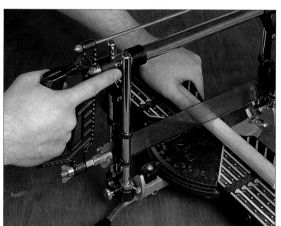

FIG 2

3 Calculate the number of pegs and cut one to length (see Fig 2). Measure this one, mark it for use as your pattern, then use the pattern as a template. These pegs are cut to 150 mm, which projects past the front of the shelf, but you can cut yours shorter, giving you more pegs per length of dowel. It is probably inadvisable to make the pegs any shorter than 80 mm.

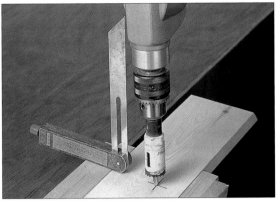

FIG 3

4 Mark out the position of the pegs at your chosen centres, with the hole centres a little below the centre line of the face side. Hold a peg in place and visually adjust the angle that you want the peg to incline. Check that you will have enough space to clear the underside of the shelf; 35 mm is an average. Secure the workpiece, use a sliding bevel set to the angle of incline of the pegs as a guide, and then drill the peg holes (see Fig 3) using a hole cutter or a flat bit drill. As you drill, be careful of any splitting out at the back.

FIG 5

6 Be careful that you do not tap the wedges too hard, otherwise you may split the end grain of the peg further than the face of the support. Leave the glue to dry, preferably overnight, then use a saw to cut the peg and wedges almost flush with the rear face. Finish by planing the peg and wedges flush to the back of the support with a block plane (see Fig 5). As always when planing end grain, apply pressure to the toe of the block plane and make sure that the blade is very sharp before you start.

FIG 4

5 Smear each peg with a little glue and insert it into the hole. Let the peg pass through the back of the support until the lower edge just meets the rear face. Ensure that the peg is supported underneath and sharply tap the end grain with a chisel. This will split the peg, allowing you to knock in a small, shallow hardwood wedge, as shown in Fig 4.

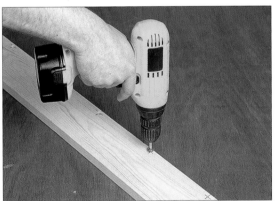

FIG 6

7 Drill and countersink the shelf components through the back edge at a regular centre of about 400 mm (see Fig 6). Match each shelf to its support, glue along the edge of the support and fasten with 50 mm screws. Keep the two parts together at 90 degrees, and be careful that the screws do not come through the face or the back of the support. Sand lightly, then prime.

Coffee table

This table is very much a modernist design, with the only decoration being in the materials. Note that the tapered legs have a line in the grain which runs through all four legs and is ranged in the same direction. It is this attention to detail that can enhance your own furniture. The proportions are of paramount importance here, and the design will not respond well to adaptation unless the whole balance is reworked.

The board material is maple-veneered MDF (medium-density fibreboard), with edging strip ironed on to the exposed edges. The legs are solid timber, biscuit-jointed to the underside of the table, and the boards are also biscuit-jointed. Finish the table with clear varnish or cellulose as the surface will need a good protection, especially on the edges.

Essential Tools

pencil, tape, square, marking knife, ruler, circular saw,
electric planer, biscuit jointer and 38 size 20 biscuits,
12 mm bevel-edge chisel, jack plane, block plane,
cabinet scraper, domestic iron, workbench, G-cramps

OTHER USEFUL TOOLS
table-mounted circular saw, palm sander

Coffee table

If you dent the veneer, apply a damp rag to the dent. This causes the wood to swell, and in most cases will remove all signs of damage.

board 20 mm

445 mm

1170 mm

505 mm

110 mm

75 x 75 mm

50 mm

35 x 35 mm

230 mm

You'll need
to know

PREPARING WOOD
p. 16

PLANING
p. 18

BISCUIT JOINTER
p. 8

Materials

2 pieces 1170 x 445 x 20 mm maple-veneered MDF

3 pieces 110 x 445 x 20 mm maple-veneered MDF

4 pieces 230 x 75 x 75 mm maple

10 m maple iron-on edging strip

sandpaper grades 150, 180, 280, 320 and 400

two-part epoxy wood glue

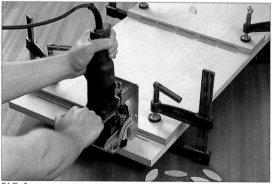

FIG 1

FIG 2

1 Mark out the boards, using a knife to cut through the veneer; make two cuts for each saw cut separated by the width of the kerf, to avoid splitting the veneer. Lay the uprights across the bottom shelf, clamped as shown in Fig 1. Cut the slots for the bottom shelf, and repeat the process for the top.

2 When preparing the maple for the legs, you need four lengths cut exactly to 230 mm. Mark the lengths with a knife and cut the barest distance from each knife cut, then use a sharp block plane to get the tops and bottoms perfectly flat and square (see Fig 2). As you plane, you will begin to see the knife cuts appear on the surface; don't plane below them.

FIG 3

3 Mark each leg with a centre line marked on all four faces and both ends, as shown in Fig 3. The taper runs from the full width of 75 mm down to 35 mm. Mark out the positions of the legs, 50 mm in from the front and back edges and 70 mm in from the ends on the underside of the table base.

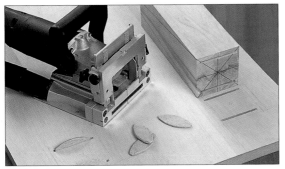

FIG 4

4 Clamp each leg up to the inner mark, ensuring that it is parallel to the edge of the base. Set the jointer plate to size 20 and cut the inner slot in both the leg and base (see Fig 4). Turn the leg around and repeat for the outer side. Repeat for each leg.

5 Remove the legs and cut the waste, as shown in Fig 5. If you have a table saw with a 75 mm or better depth of cut, this is a straightforward operation; however, you may have to remove the waste by plane or even by two passes through a smaller saw. Bring the legs to a smooth finish with a plane, and then finally use a cabinet scraper. Use the offcuts to hold the legs in the vice.

FIG 6

6 To apply the iron-on strip to the edges, set the iron to medium and apply firm pressure, checking that the glue has melted before moving on (see Fig 6). Use a block plane to remove the excess edging strip.

FIG 7

7 Use a palm sander to finish prior to assembly (see Fig 7). Glue the top first: place three bearers over the uprights top and bottom, then clamp the ends of the bearers. When gluing the legs, the weight of the table is sufficient to dispense with cramps.

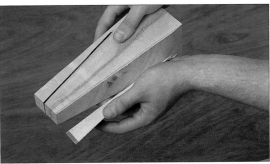

FIG 5

Computer workstation

This simple workstation, within the capabilities of even the newest weekend carpenter, is constructed from MDF (medium-density fibreboard) held together with simple plastic corner joints; you could use plywood if you wish. The rigidity comes from the two shelves fitted at a low level, providing additional storage space for paper and files. An added luxury on this version is the retractable shelf for the mouse mat; it isn't essential, but it does free up desk space.

This workstation is designed to be placed in a corner of a room that is uninterrupted by doors or low-level windows. However, your requirements may well be different, so adjust the overall dimensions to suit. Another variable is the dimensions of your computer system. Most systems are fairly standard, consisting of a monitor, keyboard, the main housing, usually a tower, a printer and a scanner or fax. Measure your system before you begin to avoid problems, and if you're making this for a friend or a relative, check the dimensions of their system first.

No glue is used in the construction, allowing you to disassemble the finished workstation and transport it as a somewhat bulky flat pack.

Essential Tools

pencil, straightedge, tape, square, screwdriver, jigsaw,
electric drill, 3 mm twist bit, block plane, workbench,
face mask

OTHER USEFUL TOOLS
table-mounted circular saw

Computer workstation

The simple plastic corner joints that provide the support
for the MDF pieces are available in packs from DIY stores.

**You'll need
to know**

FIXINGS & FITTINGS
p. 14

PREPARING WOOD
p. 16

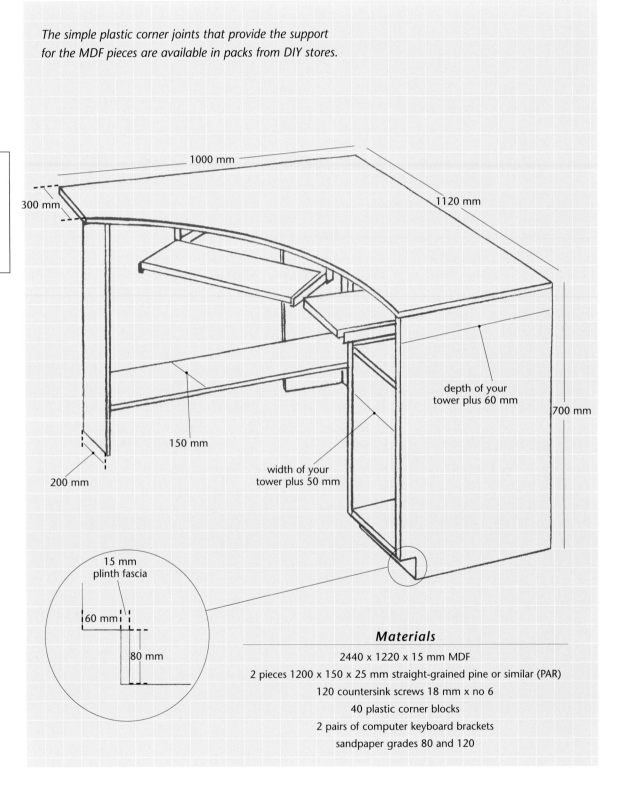

1000 mm

1120 mm

300 mm

700 mm

depth of your
tower plus 60 mm

150 mm

width of your
tower plus 50 mm

200 mm

15 mm
plinth fascia

60 mm

80 mm

Materials

2440 x 1220 x 15 mm MDF

2 pieces 1200 x 150 x 25 mm straight-grained pine or similar (PAR)

120 countersink screws 18 mm x no 6

40 plastic corner blocks

2 pairs of computer keyboard brackets

sandpaper grades 80 and 120

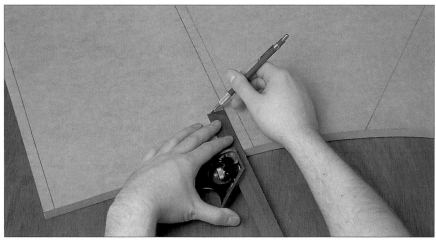

TIP

For the height of the upper shelf, an A4 folder plus 10 mm is used here. Consider how you will use the shelf and adjust it accordingly.

FIG 1

1 Measure from the best corner of the sheet of MDF how far you want to come out in both directions and mark a line square to the edge, running forward from those points. Referring to the picture on page 216, the side that the fax machine sits on should be about 300 mm long, but the other side that will house the tower needs to be the full depth of your tower plus 60 mm to allow for plugs and any cabling. Ascertain the width of your tower, add 50 mm and two thicknesses of the MDF for the uprights. Mark another square line forward at this point. Square across to form a rectangle, which is the overall size of the tower housing. From the inner corner of this rectangle to the forward point of the 300 mm line is the springing point for the front curve. Draw this freehand with a soft pencil; don't make the curve too sharp, otherwise it may partially obstruct the keyboard. Move the sheet so that the top can be cut out with a jigsaw.

2 Ensure that the workpiece is well supported at both ends, and start the cut from the 300 mm line. A table-mounted circular saw makes the job easy. When you get to the inner corner of the tower housing, stop and cut from the other edge, using a straightedge as a guide. You can now mark out for the sides of the tower housing on the underside, as shown in Fig 1. Set your combination square to 60 mm, and mark the front and back for the positions of the corner blocks. Screw the corner blocks for the tower housing in place, ensuring that they sit exactly on the line, as shown in Fig 2.

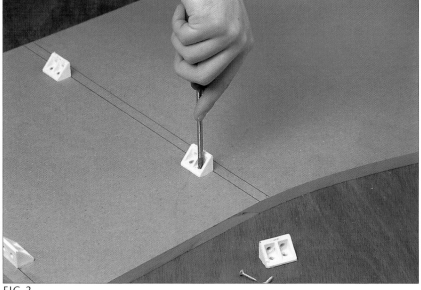

FIG 2

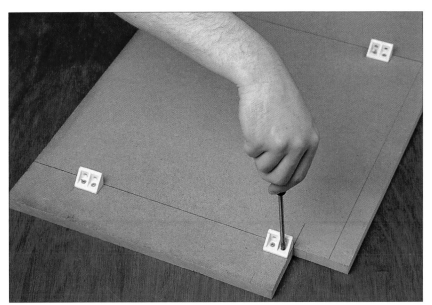

FIG 3

3 Mark out a left-hand and a right-hand side for your tower housing. The depth will be as pre-determined by the marking-out on the top, while the height will be 685 mm. On the bottom front corners, mark out a square 75 x 80 mm for the plinth fascia. Cut the sides out, plane off the saw cuts and lay the sides down on the workbench with the back edges butted up to each other. Mark across both inside faces together, the base with the underside sitting flush with the plinth cut out, and the shelf which sits just clear of the top of your tower. Use the combination square to position the connectors. Cut out two shelves, the widths determined by the marking-out on the top, and screw in place using four blocks per shelf (see Fig 3). For the plinth face, cut a strip 80 mm by the full width of the tower housing. Turn the housing upside down, and use a further two blocks to fix in place. Fix the unit to the top.

4 For the legs, cut three pieces of 685 x 200 mm and join two of them together using two blocks placed 60 mm in from the ends to provide the corner leg. A further centre block is used to provide additional support for the upper shelf; screw it in place when the shelf height has been determined (see Fig 4). Screw the corner leg to the top, coming forward about 50 mm from the edges to allow the passage of cabling behind. Place the end leg in from the back the same distance and about 75 mm from the end.

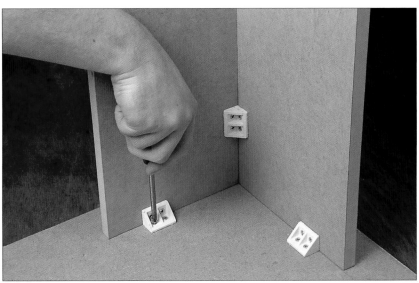

FIG 4

5 Cut the 150 x 25 mm pine to length for the shelves. The exact measurement is taken in situ, ensuring that the legs are square to the top. The upper shelf is fixed in place first. Mark the height (see Tip on page 219) on the inside face of the corner leg and on the inner face of the tower housing, fix two connector plates at each end and a further one at the same height to join the centre of the corner leg together. The underside height of the bottom shelf is the top of the lower corner block. Transfer this measurement to the single leg, fix the blocks in place and then fit the shelves, as shown in Fig 5.

FIG 5

6 Cut two pieces of MDF to the overall size of your keyboard and mouse mat, screw the sliders onto the edges, and fit the brackets that lower the sliders (see Fig 6). These generally have two positions; choose the upper for the keyboard and the lower for the mouse mat, giving clearance for the mouse when the slider is closed. Centre the keyboard on the curve and screw it into place. If you are using a mouse mat shelf, you will have to remove the top shelf of the tower housing to fix the mouse mat slider in place. Get help to turn the desk the right way up, and sand all edges prior to painting.

> **TIP**
>
> If you are making this workstation for home use, you will probably not need to change the size of your computer housing frequently. If you are thinking of constructing it for office use, however, be aware that styles and sizes of housing change with alarming frequency.

FIG 6

CD rack

Joinery shops sometimes sell offcuts of prepared hardwood. If they have been commissioned to make a piece of furniture in an exotic timber, there is always a small amount of waste left over. If you can lay your hands on a piece such as this, this CD rack is a useful and elegant item to make from it.

You will need a router, although you could cut the slots by hand and remove the waste with a chisel. If you are new to using a router, this project will introduce you to using templates and a template guide bush fitted to the base of your router.

Like the Computer workstation project on page 216, the CD rack lends itself to a degree of personalizing. The number of CDs in your collection, the different thicknesses of those CDs and your preferences for storing them (if you have a vast collection, you may want a wider rack, allowing you to store two or more rows of CDs side by side) are all worth considering. Once it is finished, coat the rack with beeswax balsam or Danish oil, either of which will provide a beautiful lustre to the wood.

Essential Tools
---

pencil, straightedge, tape, square, screwdriver, electric drill, drill bits to suit the mirror plate holes, 25 mm gouge, 12 mm and 25 mm bevel-edge chisels, router with 6 mm and 12 mm straight cutters, block plane, cabinet scraper, workbench

CD rack

You'll need to know

FIXINGS & FITTINGS p. 14

ROUTING pp. 19–21

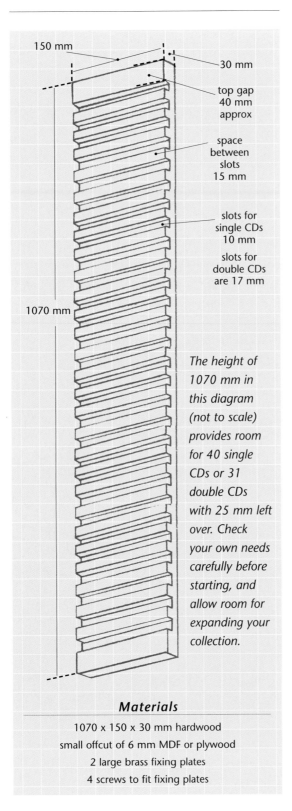

150 mm

30 mm

top gap 40 mm approx

space between slots 15 mm

slots for single CDs 10 mm

slots for double CDs are 17 mm

1070 mm

The height of 1070 mm in this diagram (not to scale) provides room for 40 single CDs or 31 double CDs with 25 mm left over. Check your own needs carefully before starting, and allow room for expanding your collection.

Materials

1070 x 150 x 30 mm hardwood
small offcut of 6 mm MDF or plywood
2 large brass fixing plates
4 screws to fit fixing plates

FIG 1

1 Choose the face of the timber with the most attractive graining and smooth it with a cabinet scraper. Clamp the wood securely and draw the scraper towards you, slightly flexing across the width of the blade as you pull (see Fig 1). Some find it more comfortable to push the scraper away from them; it doesn't matter as long as you remove the surface and are left with a silky-smooth face.

FIG 2

2 Determine the number of 10 mm slots and the number of wider ones for double or boxed set CDs. Mark out across the face of the board, leaving a gap of 15 mm between each slot and a gap of about 40 mm at the top. Use a sharp craft knife or a marking knife held firmly against a square (see Fig 2). Choose a guide bush with a hole wide enough to allow the passage of the cutter you will be using. To cut the 10 mm slots, make two passes with a 6 mm cutter. For the wider slots, make two passes with a 12 mm cutter. The bush outside diameter is 17 mm.

FIG 3

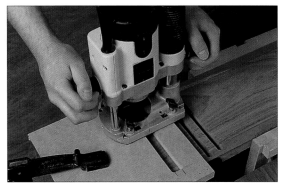

FIG 4

3 To mark and cut out your template requires a degree of precision and care. Measure the outer diameter of the guide and subtract the diameter of the cutter, then divide by 2 to give the offset from the bush to the groove you will cut. Add this measurement to the thickness of your slot, in this case 10 mm (see Fig 3). If you have a 10 mm cutter, you will only need to clamp a simple guide template the distance of the offset from one side of the cut line. If you have to do two passes, the offset needs to be added twice. Mark two parallel lines that distance apart, for instance 21 mm, as shown in the diagram below. The length of these lines should be 10 mm longer than the width of your timber at each end. Remove the waste from the template using your router fitted with a fence, taking great care that your cuts are true and do not go over the lines. When cutting with a router, follow the manufacturer's operating and safety instructions at all times, even for what might appear to be simple cuts.

4 Fit the guide bush to the base of your router. Clamp the work together firmly in your vice, clamp the MDF (medium-density fibreboard) template in place centred over your knife marks, and make a practice pass with the bit lowered to just above the face of the work. Do not turn the router on for this pass, but look at the cutter carefully to ensure that it will not go past your marks. When you are sure everything is OK cut the slot, lowering the cutter a little more each pass to avoid any burning. Move the template along the workpiece to the next slot, ensuring that everything is stable and firmly clamped as you go (see Fig 4).

FIG 5

5 When all the slots have been cut, turn the timber over in the vice and place the fixing plates in position. These are ordinary brass fixing plates rebated into the rear surface. When positioning them, ensure that the fixing screws are not in line with a slot on the face, but are lined up with one of the gaps (see Fig 5). Using an 18 mm gouge will speed up this process.

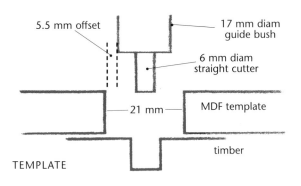

5.5 mm offset

17 mm diam guide bush

6 mm diam straight cutter

21 mm — MDF template

timber

TEMPLATE

Letter box

This project introduces cold-form bending, a technique that can, in relatively small projects, replace specialized steam bending; even better, unlike steam bending, it requires no expensive equipment. It also uses the fillet joint – a bead of viscous epoxy glue smeared across two adjacent surfaces, with the bead providing the actual joint. It is stronger than the timber it joins and has no loss of strength when used as a gap-filling compound up to 6 mm wide. Here, it is used to join the roof to the carcass.

To construct the roof, use layers of thin plywood or veneers built up to a thickness of 8 mm. Paper-backed veneers, which are cheap and don't tear or split along the grain, are ideal. Since only small amounts are needed for this project, see if any local cabinet-makers or joinery shops have some offcuts.

The letter box here was fully veneered with maple, but you can stain or paint the carcass and use aero or skin plywood for the roof. This is a flexible plywood thinner than 2 mm that will bend to a radius of less than 100 mm. The finish is two-pack polyurethane matt varnish, with the inside painted with bright red eggshell.

——— Essential Tools ———

pencil, tape, square, sliding bevel, Flexicurve or French curves, craft knife or scalpel, jigsaw, electric drill, 2 mm, 4 mm and 6 mm wood bits, belt sander, 12 mm and 25 mm bevel-edge chisels, jack plane, block plane, workbench, G-cramps

Letter box

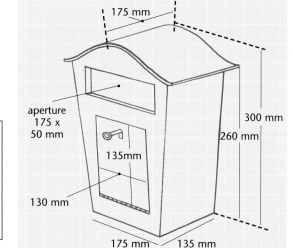

175 mm

aperture
175 x
50 mm

300 mm

260 mm

135mm

130 mm

175 mm · 135 mm

**You'll need
to know**

FIXINGS & FITTINGS
p. 14

SAWS
pp. 6–10

Materials

650 x 435 x 9 mm exterior-grade plywood

650 x 435 mm sheet of paper-backed veneer (optional)

650 x 650 mm sheet of paper-backed veneer or
aero/skin plywood

1000 x 75 x 50 mm sawn pine or similar

130 mm brass or stainless steel piano hinge and screws

small brass cabinet lock and screws

sandpaper grades 100 to 240

PVA wood glue

two-part epoxy glue and colloidal silica

1 Cut three 330 mm lengths of 75 x 50 mm timber, plane or belt-sand the faces smooth, and select one block as a pattern. Mark the centre line and two square lines 300 mm apart, and use a Flexicurve or French curve to draw a slow curve with a slight upstand at the ends. The curve should lie roughly in the centre of the block. Cut to the line with a jigsaw. If the blade wanders during cutting, correct this with a belt sander. Use the pattern to replicate the marks on the other two blocks.

2 Glue each set of three formers together with PVA, then clamp and leave to dry. Cut the 9 mm ply to the sizes prescribed while the blocks are drying. Plane a bevel on the two short sides of the base, making the angle the same as the sides. Fit each half of the completed block in the vice and use a belt sander to obtain a good fit of the two parts. Ensure that the two surfaces not only fit but that they are as near as possible square to the edges.

FIG 1

3 Cut the skin plywood or veneer into eight sheets of 160 x 320 mm, four sheets running with the grain and four against. Place a sheet of newspaper over the concave section of the block and lay each sheet of veneer in place, alternating the grain direction. Lay a further sheet of newspaper over the final sheet, place the convex block in place and apply hand pressure. Check that each sheet of veneer is tightly compressed up against its neighbour and that you have an equal amount of overhang at each end. Unpack the stack and lay aside in reverse order. Mix the epoxy glue – with a 5:1 ratio you will need about 20 ml of resin and 4 ml of fast hardener. Wear gloves, work quickly and insert both sheets of newspaper (see Fig 1). Clamp and clean off any excess glue.

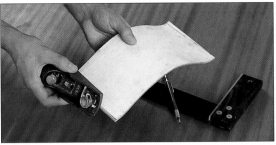

FIG 2

4 When dry – normally about two hours at 20 °C – unclamp and remove the newspaper and excess glue using a belt sander fitted with 120 grit or higher. You can accelerate the drying time by gently applying heat via a heat gun or a blow heater. Use a block plane to get the edges exactly flush, starting with the front edge, and then using a square to mark the two ends. Plane towards the centre to avoid splitting the ends (see Fig 2). Lay the edge of the roof section over the front and back walls and check the fit – 0.5 mm either way is acceptable. Sand or plane the roof line to achieve the fit.

5 Mark out the front panel to the given measurements, drill a hole in the waste parts and remove the waste with a jigsaw. Cut as close as you can with the blade and clean up with a chisel. (If you have a router, use it for this job and cut the corners of the openings square.) Test the replacement door panel for fit: you should have a gap of less than 0.5 mm all round, except for the bottom edge, which needs a gap of 4 mm to accommodate the hinge.

6 Cut the veneers, if you intend to use them. Each component will need to be cut with about a 10 mm overhang all round. If you are using paper-backed veneers for convenience, sharp scissors are the best method of cutting them. When you come to the apertures, use a sharp craft knife or a scalpel to exactly mark each corner with two right-angled cuts. Turn the veneer face up and join the marks using a steel rule, taking care not to cut past the pre-cut corners.

7 Apply glue to the veneers and clamp up; protect the veneer with paper, and don't clamp too tightly. When dry, clean up and cut the edges of the veneer flush as follows: front, back and door, all edges; sides, the top and bottom only; leave all the overhangs on the base.

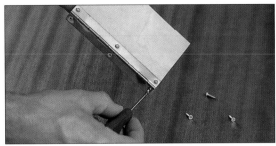

FIG 3

8 Cut the piano hinge to the same size as the bottom of the door and screw in place (see Fig 3). The centre of the knuckle should be exactly over the inner edge of the door. Screw to the front panel and plane the door if necessary.

FIG 4

9 Unscrew the door and remove the waste for the lock. Fit the lock and striking plate (see Fig 4), mark for the keyhole and cut with drills and chisel. Do not refit the door. To increase the viscosity of the glue mix and prevent it running down the joins, add up to 35% colloidal silica. When dry, shave off the overhanging veneers from the box with a block plane. Make another mix as before and glue the roof in place upside down. Pour in a generous amount of glue and use a rounded spatula to form the 6 mm fillet joint when the glue has started to cure. Replace the door and sand the box smooth.

Vanity unit

This design is influenced by the English Arts and Crafts and the French Art Nouveau movements. Although it is not a project for the beginner, providing your marking out is done with care, you should be able to produce a good-looking unit. Any reasonably stable hardwood can be used, although oak is the most stylistically correct for this type of design. The finish is a light coat of liming wax followed by a rich coat of beeswax.

When drawing out the shapes, take care that you do not make the curves too abrupt or too deep. Each curve should flow into the next. Achieving a balance for the upstand or splashback is very much a matter of trial and error. The return curves at the rear of the top have to balance with the outer edge of the upstand. The best method is to cut a template as shown on page 253; place this on the top and look hard at how the lines of the top and upstand intersect from every conceivable angle. The legs are splayed at 5 degrees from vertical – the front legs are splayed both out and forward, while the back legs only splay out.

Essential Tools
---

pencil, tape, square, marking knife, mortise gauge, screwdriver, crosscut saw, jigsaw, spokeshave, belt sander, electric drill, 5, 4 and 3 mm wood bits, countersink bit, router with 6, 12 and 25 mm straight cutters, plus a quarter-round cutter of 22 mm diameter with a 6 mm radius for the upper curve of the top and a 25 mm diameter ogee cutter with a 3 mm radius for the underside, biscuit jointer and 10 size 20 biscuits, range of bevel-edge chisels, jack plane, block plane, cabinet scraper, workbench, sash cramps

OTHER USEFUL TOOLS
table-mounted circular saw, electric hand plane, bandsaw

Vanity unit

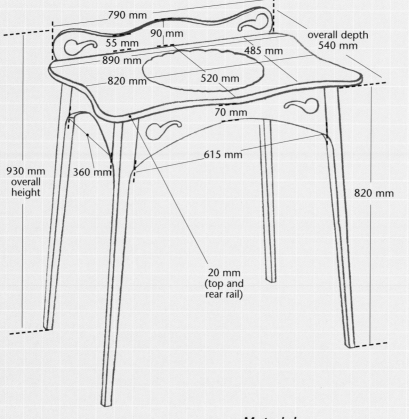

790 mm

90 mm

55 mm

890 mm

820 mm

485 mm

520 mm

overall depth
540 mm

70 mm

615 mm

930 mm
overall
height

360 mm

820 mm

20 mm
(top and
rear rail)

*Do not use steel or
brass-plated screws in
oak, as they cause
severe discoloration of
the timber; instead, use
solid brass screws.
Always cut the screw
hole with a steel screw
of the same size first,
withdraw the steel
screw and replace with
a brass one.*

**You'll need
to know**

PREPARING WOOD
p. 16

PLANING
p. 18

JOINTS
pp. 18–21

Materials

4 pieces 850 x 60 x 60 mm American white oak (legs)

850 x 170 x 35 mm American white oak (front rail)

2 pieces 420 x 170 x 35 mm American white oak (side rails)

700 x 100 x 20 mm American white oak (rear rail)

2700 (3 x 900) x 200 x 20 mm American white oak (top)

800 x 100 x 20 mm American white oak (upstand)

4 brass countersink screws 50 mm x no 10

18 brass roundhead screws 18 mm x no 6

6 stretcher plates

sandpaper grades 100 to 400

waterproof wood glue (Cascamite or similar)

1 Plane the legs true, 60 mm square and 850 mm long. When selecting the face and face-edge marks, bear in mind that the legs will splay out, so use the grain pattern to accentuate this if possible. If you use an electric plane, as shown in Fig 1, never plane closer than about 0.5 mm from the finished line, and keep your hand well away from the blades. Always finish with a jack plane, as this gives greater control and a far superior finish.

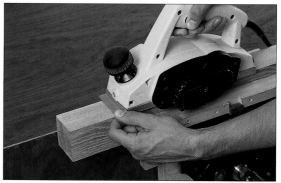

FIG 1

FIG 2

2 Select the legs according to grain type and direction for the best location, front or back pair, and mark accordingly. For the front pair, mark an 85-degree compound bevel with the lowest point being the front, outer corner (see Fig 2). For the rear legs, mark a simple bevel with the lower portion on the outer faces. For the front rail mortise, mark 12 mm with a mortise gauge 11.5 mm in from the front face. Cut all eight mortises using a router with a 12 mm straight cutter, except for the two inner faces of the back legs; these are cut to 6 mm wide and 7 mm in from the rear face. Set the depth of cut to maximum – using standard straight cutters this is 30 mm, and is just about sufficient.

FIG 3

3 Fig 3 shows the front left leg being marked for the curve between the upper end of the taper and the shoulder line of the front rail on the inner face. Repeat these markings on the front face and then for the other three legs. (The back legs should be marked on the inner and rear faces.)

4 The taper is marked out as in the diagram on page 253 – remember that the upper thickness, from whence the curve springs, is 40 mm. Make sure that the marks are on the prescribed faces, otherwise you will remove one set of marks when you cut the tapers.

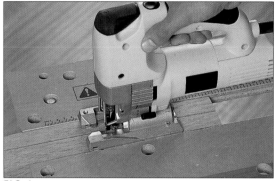
FIG 4

5 To remove the waste from the legs, use a jigsaw with the work mounted as shown in Fig 4. Move the leg along the workbench as you proceed, to ensure you do not bind the saw blade. After the first cut rotate the leg through 90 degrees and use the non-parallel jaws of the workbench to secure the job. Do not cut close to the line, especially when negotiating the curve – no matter how good the jigsaw, a small amount of wander on the blade is inevitable. If you have access to a bandsaw, use it for this step.

FIG 5

6 Any error in the cut of the inner faces of the legs can be removed with a spokeshave or a belt sander, using the "nose" of the tool to finish the curve.

7 Mount the legs in a vice or workbench, as shown in Fig 5, and plane the inside corner down to the 35 mm marks. This will leave a triangle reminiscent of a Gothic arch. Draw a line joining the two 35 mm marks across the face of the triangle and use a belt sander to remove the timber up to the line. The curved triangle that will result should be continued down the inner corner of the leg, feathering out about 100 mm below the shoulder lines. Mount each leg vertically in the vice and remove the end-grain waste down to the bevel marks, the bulk with the belt sander, finishing off with a block plane. Finish all faces of the legs with a cabinet scraper.

FIG 6

8 Cut the four rails to the sizes on page 232 – these are overlong, but will be cut to the correct length when the leg bevels have been marked. For the front rail, mark 615 mm along the upper edge, then lay the sliding bevel, set to 85 degrees, on the lower edge and mark with a knife. Slide the bevel along the length of the tenons – 30 mm unless you have cut the leg mortises deeper – and mark another line at each end. Square all lines around the rail, using the bevel and a square. Repeat for the smaller section rear rail. The side rails are 360 mm shoulder to shoulder, with the difference that the rear shoulder will be square to the upper edge; add the length of the tenons and cut to size. Clamp a batten parallel to the shoulder offset by the distance of the edge of your router to the edge of a 25 mm straight cutter, and remove the cheeks of the tenons (see Fig 6).

9 Cut away the excess portions – for the large tenons, 35 mm from the top and 20 mm from the bottom, for the smaller tenons on the rear rail, 25 mm from the top and 20 mm from the bottom. The measurements are taken from the shoulder line and are marked at 90 degrees to the shoulder, not the edge. Round off the edges of the tenons to fit the mortises, clean up the shoulders and assemble.

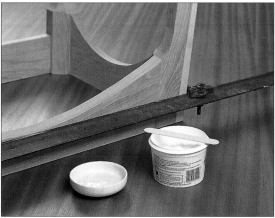

FIG 7

10 Once you have a good fit with all the shoulders meeting the legs, mark the top of the rails to replicate the bevels on the legs, disassemble and plane in the vice, checking the angle by using the sliding bevel. Before disassembling, make a small mark where the curve of each leg meets the adjacent rail. Once the top bevels have been planed, mark the centre of the front and side faces, measure down 70 mm for the front and 75 mm for the sides and mark. Use a long steel ruler to achieve a smooth curve between the three points. Draw the curve with a pencil, then remove the waste with a jigsaw. Reassemble and check that the flow of the leg curves into the rails and that the top bevel is flat all the way across the table. Cut six slow wedges from scrap and glue up, as shown in Fig 7. Don't place the cramp higher than shown, or you may shear the short grain on the curve of rail where it meets the leg. Tighten all cramps, check that the interior is square and clean up.

FIG 8

FIG 9

11 Cut the three parts for the top to 900 mm. Arrange them side by side, with the grain cupped alternately to minimize warping. Place any knots or defects in the centre, where you will cut out for the basin. Biscuit-joint the pieces, glue up and clamp together. When dry, place on the leg assembly with a 20 mm overhang to the rear and sketch out the edge profile, using a soft pencil. To achieve perfect symmetry, draw one half, trace it, flip the tracing paper and then press into the grain through the trace onto the other side with a hard pencil. Cut to the line with a jigsaw, smooth off with a belt sander, then rout the profile with a quarter-round cutter for the top edge and an ogee cutter for the bottom edge (see Fig 8), leaving a small return of about 3 mm at the base.

12 Sketch out the profile of the upstand on a 800 x 100 mm offcut of MDF (medium-density fibreboard) or plywood. Use the front edge of the top as a template, reducing the length by 18 mm at each end. Place the template in position and adjust your lines as required. When you are satisfied with the shape, cut it out with a jigsaw and look at it in place again. If you're unsure that each side is symmetrical, use the best end, mark the centre and flip the template over.

13 Transfer the template to the upstand (splashback), as shown in Fig 9, and cut out. Drill four countersunk holes from the underside of the top to fix in place, but do not fit yet.

FIG 10

14 Lay the top upside down with the leg assembly in place and fit the stretcher plates in place (see Fig 10). They will need to be bent slightly to accommodate the angled rails. Use only the slots that traverse the grain, as any expansion or contraction takes place across the width of timber, not the length. Place the screws in the centre of each slot. Turn upright, and screw and glue the upstand in place. Place the completed table on a flat, level surface, scribe around the base of each leg and cut to the line with a tenon saw. Then lay the ceramic basin upside down in place and draw round the rim, subtract the width of the rim and draw a second inner circle; cut to this second line and fit the basin with a bead of silicone mastic.

TIP

Longer straight cutters, called pocket cutters, are available for cutting deeper mortises.

Tall storage chest

This project takes the weekend carpenter on to the next level: simple cabinet-making. To construct the drawers, a professional, full-size dovetail jig is used here; smaller jigs with a cutting width of up to 300 mm are also available. Look for rigidity in the plate, and ensure that the guide bush will fit your router. The jig should be mounted on a ply or MDF (medium-density fibreboard) base, with a 25 mm hole drilled to a depth of 25 mm in one overhanging end to receive the protruding cutter when not being used for machining. The front of the drawer is placed face down on the top of the jig, with the relevant side mounted vertically in place. The off-set, which enables the pins and sockets of the dovetail to align, is achieved by using a small pin that screws into the side of the jig.

If you do not have access to a good-quality table saw and thicknesser, get the timbers prepared to size at a yard or joinery shop. Ash, the cheapest hardwood at the time of writing, is used here. However, it tends to tear along the grain, so keep your tools perfectly honed and expect to spend some time finishing with the cabinet scraper.

——— Essential Tools ———

pencil, steel rule or tape, square, marking knife, coping saw, drill with 3 mm and 4 mm twist bits, countersink bit, circular saw, router with 6 mm straight cutter and 45-degree bevel cutter, dovetail cutting jig and 11 mm dovetail cutter, biscuit jointer, 28 size 10 and 50 size 20 biscuits, range of bevel-edge chisels, jack plane, block plane, cabinet scraper, framing cramps, sash cramps or cramp heads, workbench

OTHER USEFUL TOOLS
table-mounted circular saw, electric hand plane

Tall storage chest

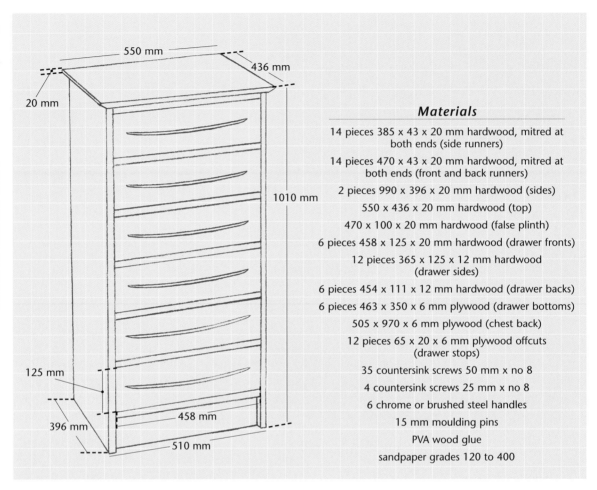

550 mm

436 mm

20 mm

1010 mm

125 mm

396 mm

458 mm

510 mm

You'll need
to know

PREPARING WOOD
p. 16

ROUTING
pp. 19–21

CUTTING MITRES
p. 21

Materials

14 pieces 385 x 43 x 20 mm hardwood, mitred at
both ends (side runners)

14 pieces 470 x 43 x 20 mm hardwood, mitred at
both ends (front and back runners)

2 pieces 990 x 396 x 20 mm hardwood (sides)

550 x 436 x 20 mm hardwood (top)

470 x 100 x 20 mm hardwood (false plinth)

6 pieces 458 x 125 x 20 mm hardwood (drawer fronts)

12 pieces 365 x 125 x 12 mm hardwood
(drawer sides)

6 pieces 454 x 111 x 12 mm hardwood (drawer backs)

6 pieces 463 x 350 x 6 mm plywood (drawer bottoms)

505 x 970 x 6 mm plywood (chest back)

12 pieces 65 x 20 x 6 mm plywood offcuts
(drawer stops)

35 countersink screws 50 mm x no 8

4 countersink screws 25 mm x no 8

6 chrome or brushed steel handles

15 mm moulding pins

PVA wood glue

sandpaper grades 120 to 400

FIG 1

1 Prepare the timber as per the cutting list; cut the top and sides to length and biscuit-joint them along the edges. Arrange all the mitre-cut runners on edge, with the shorter edge upper-most. Make a mark across the end grain 20 mm away from the short point at both ends, as shown

upper left in Fig 1: use one of the runners as a guide stick, hold it in place across all the mitres and then mark along the underside with a pencil. On the shorter side runners, mark and drill two 4 mm diameter countersunk holes, 50 mm in from the short point of the mitres, (see centre in Fig 1). Sort the runners into seven sets of four, two sides and a front and back, and cut a slot into the edge of the mitres for a size 10 biscuit, using the end-grain mark as a register mark for the jointer. Ensure that the work is securely clamped or that you screw the jointer to the workbench and use a fixed stop. The small amount of breakout on the short point, where the end of the biscuit will show, will not be seen and can be removed with a coping saw later.

2 Glue and clamp each frame, lay it flat with all glue wiped off, and ensure that it is perfectly square before leaving to dry.

FIG 2

3 When dry, release the frames and number them 1 to 7, on the back edge with each frame's best face up. Check that they are uniform, and if necessary plane the outer edges until they are all the same width and all square to the front edge. Stack the frames, ensuring that they are flat and level. Cut 12 offcuts of plywood into small trapezia, as shown in Fig 2; to form drawer stops. Glue and pin them in place to the six lower frames, with the front edge of the plywood back 20 mm from the front edge of the frame, i.e. the thickness of the drawer fronts.

FIG 3

4 Fig 3 shows two drawer fronts mounted face down in the dovetail jig, with the thinner sides clamped face in. Ensure that the parts are cut perfectly square and the side is flush to the upper face of the front. When you place the fronts in position, check that what will be the top edge of the drawer will have a pin and not a socket. Adjust this by moving the work to the left or right.

5 Mount the guide bush that comes with the template on the underside of your router, push the plunger down and lock off. Insert the dovetail bit and adjust the depth to 11 mm. Be careful not to inadvertently release the plunge lock when setting the fine depth adjuster, or when you finish a pass – if you do, especially when the router is running, you will ruin both cutter and guide bush.

FIG 4

6 Insert the dovetail template in place, using the adjustment nuts to achieve an exact alignment of the cutting line on the template surface with the join between the front and side parts of the drawer, and start to machine. Always work from left to right, allowing the router to achieve full speed prior to entry, and make the cuts through both pieces of timber (see Fig 4).

FIG 5

7 Fig 5 shows clearly a fully machined joint still clamped in the jig and an exploded joint that demonstrates how the workpieces should look when you have finished the cut.

FIG 6

8 To cut a groove for the drawer bottoms, fit a 6 mm straight cutter to your router and set the depth of cut to 5 mm, with the distance on the fence 8 mm in from the bottom edge of the drawer sides and fronts (see Fig 6). These grooves or housings should stop short on both ends of the front by 5 mm. Square off the end of these housings with a 6 mm chisel. The sides can be routed the full length, as the housing will fall in line with the lowest socket, provided you have mounted the fronts correctly in the jig (see step 4).

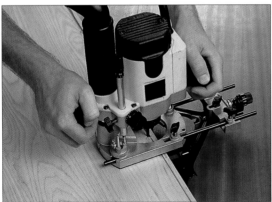

FIG 7

9 While the router is set up, rout out the carcass sides for the plywood back at this stage. As before, cut a 6 mm groove 5 mm deep, but this time adjust the fence to cut 5 mm in from the rear edge, as shown in Fig 7. Run the groove the entire length of both sides. Take care that the fence is parallel at the start and finish of each pass.

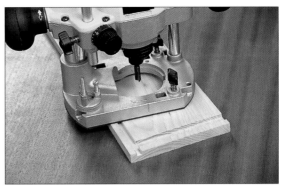

FIG 8

10 Cut a housing to the same depth, 12 mm wide, taken from 10 mm in from the end of the drawer sides and stopped at the 6 mm housing for the drawer bottom (see Fig 8). You can either use a 12 mm straight cutter or make two passes with the 6 mm one. Clamp a guide batten across the timber or use the router's fence across the end of the drawer side – the latter is far quicker, but take extreme care that the router doesn't "rock in" when starting the cut. Cabinet-scrape and sand all the inner faces of the drawers.

FIG 9

11 Glue up the drawers upside down, as shown in Fig 9. This allows you to check the positioning of the drawer back, and in addition will stop the back from sliding down the housing. Note that the glue blocks are pulled back from the drawer front to allow the dovetails to pull up tightly.

FIG 10

12 When fitting the bottoms to the drawers, you may need to use a block plane to achieve a slight bevel on the underside of the plywood. Glue each bottom in the grooves and pin the back edge to the underside of the drawer back (see Fig 10). Stack all the drawers interspersed with the frames on a level surface, check for any errors, especially on the width of the drawers, and rectify as required. No drawer should be narrower than the frames – if they are, you will once again have to plane the widths of the frames. Number the drawers on the back.

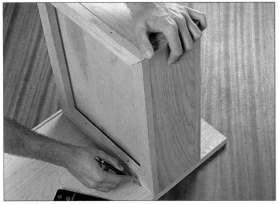

FIG 11

13 Lay one side down on the bench and, starting at the top, mark the position of each frame and drawer (see Fig 11), ensuring that they are square to the front edge of the side. Run a bead of glue where the frames lie, use a 3 mm drill bit to start the screws, and screw the six lower frames in place. Turn the assembly over and lay it on the other side of the carcass.

FIG 12

14 Repeat step 12 for the other side, checking continually that the carcass doesn't shift to a parallelogram (see Fig 12). When satisfied, leave to dry, lying on its back. Use a bevel cutter with a guide wheel to bevel the underside edge of the top. Cut to a depth of 14 mm on the front and both sides, leaving the back edge as is. Place the top on the carcass and centre it, which should leave a 20 mm overhang all round. Mark the position of the top frame from the inside of the carcass. Glue and screw the final frame to the top, making sure that the front overhang is correctly positioned. Replace the top on the carcass and screw and glue top in place via the frame sides.

FIG 13

15 Fit each drawer to its opening, planing the sides of the drawer where necessary and using a block plane to round the rear ends of each drawer side. Use a piece of thin card to achieve a consistent gap all the way around the drawer front (Fig 13). Fit the handles; insert and pin the back as for the drawer bottoms. Screw the false plinth using two blocks set back 40 mm from the front edge of the carcass.

Kitchen unit makeover

You can transform most kitchens with a little time, money and ingenuity. This "makeover" retains the basic kitchen unit carcass, and replaces the doors, drawer fronts and worktop with your own custom-made versions. Most fitted kitchens are made from coated chipboard, which chips easily and becomes swollen and bloated when subject to moisture. Pay special attention to the sink cupboard: you may need to replace the whole thing, in which case buy from a cheaper range and discard the doors and false drawer fronts. If any part is swollen or the coating is damaged, replace it.

All doors and drawer fronts should be replaced with painted MDF (medium-density fibreboard) or solid timber, and the work surfaces replaced with plywood covered in a waterproof material: tiles, slate, resin, or even real wood. Here, 300 mm square ceramic floor tiles are cemented to low-grade construction plywood using flexible tile cement.

The sinks are stainless steel inset bowls with a monoblock mixer tap serving both. If you need to move the sink, you will have to sort out the new feed for the taps and a waste pipe. Plan and complete any electrical work first. If you need additional sockets and have any doubt whatsoever about your competence, employ a qualified electrician.

To finish, apply eggshell paint after priming and undercoating the MDF. It's easiest to remove the doors for painting.

Essential Tools

pencil, straightedge, tape, square, screwdriver, mastic skeleton gun, panel saw, jigsaw, electric drill, 4 mm twist bit, 35 mm recessed hinge cutter, drill stand, jack plane, block plane, workbench
For cutting ceramic tiles: tile cutter, angle grinder with stone-cutting disc, hacksaw frame with ceramic cutting file fitted

OTHER USEFUL TOOLS
table-mounted or hand-held circular saw

Kitchen unit makeover

You'll need to know

FIXINGS & FITTINGS
p. 14

PREPARING WOOD
p. 16

SAWS
pp. 6–10

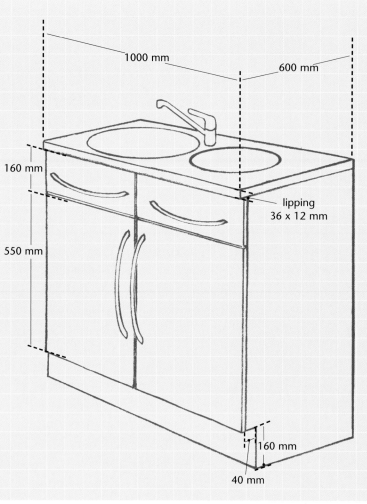

1000 mm

600 mm

160 mm

550 mm

lipping
36 x 12 mm

160 mm

40 mm

Materials

554 x 500 x 15 mm MDF per door
224 x 500 x 15 mm MDF per drawer
2440 x 1220 x 18 mm shuttering ply
2000 x 20 x 25 mm hardwood lipping
ceramic tiles and flexible tile cement
inset sink(s) and taps
drawer and door handles
silicone mastic
plastic corner blocks
30 18 mm x no 6 brass
countersink screws
sandpaper grades 80 and 100

The dimensions shown in this diagram are compatible with most self-assembly sink units available at DIY shops. You can adapt the measurements to fit existing or one-off units, but make sure that you keep everything in proportion.

WORKTOPS

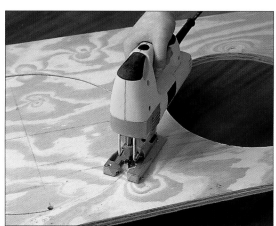

FIG 1

1 Remove the existing worktop and sink, which will be fixed by angle brackets underneath. If you have pipes running through the worktop, these will have to be cut free. Repeat the shape of the old worktop in the shuttering plywood and fit in place, using new brackets if necessary. If you need to join the plywood, make the join meet over the place where two adjacent cupboards abut. Most manufacturers provide a paper template to cut the hole(s) for a new sink; drill a small hole to start the cut and then follow the line with a jigsaw, as shown in Fig 1.

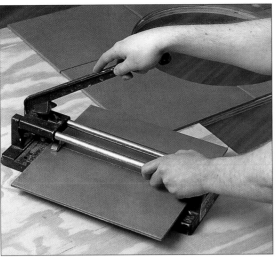

FIG 2

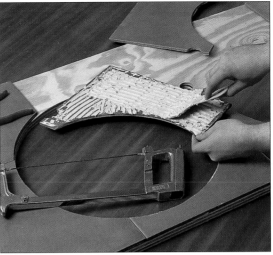

FIG 3

2 Loosely lay out the tiles on the worktop, allowing a 4 mm grout line between all joins; find a visual balance that keeps cutting to a minimum. Where possible, any cuts should be placed to the back or the sides of the worktop. It's a good idea to have a join running through where the tap hole will be. This will also give a neat line through the middle of the two sinks. Mark the tiles with a felt pen and cut them as shown in Fig 2. To cut curved tiles, transfer the sink cutout to the tile and then clamp the tile securely. Tape over the good part of the tile with masking tape to protect it should you slip, and run around the curved line with an angle grinder. If you haven't done this before, take it slowly. When you have ground down about halfway, the waste will break off and you will be left with a very sharp jagged edge. Use the grinder to smooth this off. When the tiles are cut, loose-lay them in position, check that the sink will fit and adjust if needed.

TIP

Wear gardening gloves while handling the sharp edges of tiles; this will minimize the risk of accidents.

---

3 Spread the cement evenly on the back of each tile and twist into place. Some cement manufacturers recommend trowelling the surface to be fixed to; when dealing with large tiles it is cleaner, if a little slower, to trowel onto the back of the tile (see Fig 3). Use the cement applicator to ensure an even coating. Use tile spacers or matchsticks to keep an even grout line, and continually check the surface height, tapping down or adding cement as necessary.

FIG 4

4 When the tile cement is dry, usually the following day, cut and fit the edge beading. This should be the width of the tiles plus the ply and about 8–12 mm thick. Mitre all the corners and screw in place (see Fig 4). If you wish, you can counterbore and plug the screw holes. Grout the work surface and allow it to dry.

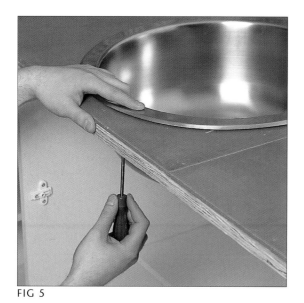

FIG 5

5 Place the sinks into the holes, seal with silicone mastic and tighten the sink clamps from underneath the worktop, according to the manufacturer's instructions (see Fig 5). As you tighten the screws, the mastic will be expelled from under the sink rim; wipe away any excess with a wet finger, using clean water from a bowl, not your saliva. Fit and connect the taps, using flexible hose connectors if you're a weekend plumber. The sink waste will need to be adapted if you are changing from one sink to a two-bowl system. A simple dimensioned sketch will be enough to solve your problem if you take it to a good plumber's merchant. Buy the push-fit waste system, not the glued type.

DRAWER FRONTS AND DOORS

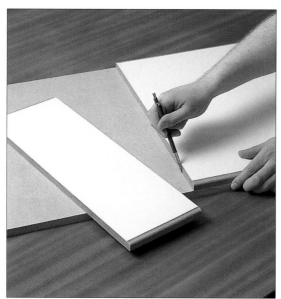

FIG 6

FIG 7

6 Remove each door and drawer from the existing units and lay it over a sheet of 15 mm MDF. Mark around each component, using the board to the most economical advantage (see Fig 6). Remember to allow for the thickness of your saw cut (the kerf) when marking. If any of your existing doors are damaged in any way, do not use them as a template, but substitute another of the same size.

7 Ensure that the board is firmly supported and fix a batten as a guide, then saw the components off, as shown in Fig 7 – using a circular saw makes the job easy. Stack them in groups of the same size, clamp in a vice and plane the edges smooth and square. You may wish to put a slight bevel on the face edges at this stage, using a block plane: about 4 mm all round looks attractive.

FIG 8

FIG 10

8 Fix a corner block at each end of the false drawer fronts (see Fig 8) and place in position on the cupboard. Inset the blocks by the thickness of the uprights, half the thickness in the centre of a double unit. Make sure that the drawer front is square and level, then screw in place. (Use a bradawl to start the screws off.) If replacing any practical (functional) drawers, simply unscrew the old front from inside the drawer and replace with your new version. With regard to fitting the doors, refer to step 10.

9 The handles used here come with a fixing template, and the only thing to be done is to choose their placing. Centre the drawer handles on the width of the drawer; a low placing looks better for the drawer handles. The door handles are placed 50 mm in from the edge and lifted towards the top, partly for ergonomic reasons and partly for a visual balance. Play around with the placing until you feel satisfied that the handles are in the best position in relation to each other. When you have decided, fix all handles in exactly the same position, ensuring that they are exactly square (see Fig 9). To cut the holes for the door hinges, see page 252, steps 7 and 8.

10 You will have to spend some time adjusting the fit of the doors; it is tedious but straightforward. There are usually two adjusting screws on each hinge: the larger allows you to move the hinge forward on the hinge backplate. By adjusting each of the pair of hinges using these screws, as shown in Fig 10, you can get the hinge edge of the door square to the edge of the cupboard. The smaller screw, often hidden inside the plastic casing, allows you to "throw the door forward", adjusting the other edge. This is important if you have a pair of doors meeting, as the gap between them must be parallel and the tops at the same height.

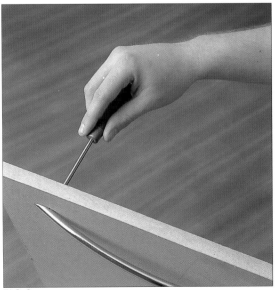

FIG 9

Wall cupboard

This project, while using a different construction method to the kitchen unit makeover on page 242, is essentially a variation on a theme. The timber used for the doors, which are hung on an existing cupboard unit, is the highly fashionable maple, which is straight-grained and satisfying to work. Low-voltage lights are mounted inside the cupboards; if you wish to do this you will need to bring an electric feed up to the top of the cupboards. The transformer can be left just sitting above the cupboard, with the fittings mounted in the top.

Glass-fronted doors are used for these cupboards. You can use glass doors fitted at low level for floor units, although these are not ideal if you have young children. Frosted glass blurs the cupboard's contents and is a compromise between to display or to conceal. If the contents are very much display items, use clear glass or, for a truly modernist look, Georgian wired safety glass.

In this project, it is assumed that you have mastered the skills required to true up your timber and that you are reasonably competent at making a mortise and tenon joint. The joint used in this door is a haunched mortise and tenon with 12 mm cut away, so that the rebate for the glass does not expose the tenon.

Essential Tools

pencil, straightedge, tape, square, marking gauge, mortise gauge, marking knife, screwdriver, jack plane, block plane, 6 mm, 12 mm and 25 mm bevel-edge chisels, mallet, tenon saw, electric drill, drill stand, 35 mm recessed hinge cutter, router, 6 mm straight cutter, 10 mm rebate cutter with guide wheel, workbench, sash cramps

OTHER USEFUL TOOLS
table-mounted circular saw

Wall cupboard

You'll need to know

PREPARING WOOD p. 16

ROUTING pp. 19–21

If you have good control of a mastic gun, it is possible to fix the glass in the cupboard doors by running a small bead of clear mastic around the inside of the glass.

The diagram below gives the correct measurements for the haunched mortise and tenon joint.

500 mm

18 mm

720 mm

65 mm

65 mm

Stile

65mm

6mm

12mm

41mm

18mm

12mm

Rail

12mm

18mm

6mm

Materials

(These quantities are for one door with a finished size of 720 x 500 mm; multiply these amounts or alter the lengths as necessary)

2 pieces 740 x 65 x 18 mm maple

2 pieces 520 x 65 x 18 mm maple

608 x 382 mm etched or sandblasted 4 mm glass

2 m x 6 mm x 6 mm hardwood fillet

moulding pins

PVA wood glue

sandpaper grades 100 to 300

FIG 1

1 First, you need to mark out a rod, a simple measuring stick with all the dimensions to be transferred to each piece of timber. Starting at one end of the rod, mark an end point. Measure from this the height of your doors and mark them for the upright pieces, called stiles. In Fig 1 the line in the foreground on the rod is the end point; next, 12 mm along, is the line marking the haunch of the tenon, then the line of the cut back for the glass rebate, and then the line for the full width of the rail that will meet up to the stile. The horizontal timbers of a door are called rails and, because they are so much shorter, you can mark them between the stile marks. Normally all marks would start from the same end point, but to avoid visual confusion, they are placed in the middle. The final line in the foreground, just in front of the square, is the length of the tenon.

2 Line up all your stiles, cut them about 30 mm longer than the finished length and transfer the marks from the rod. Repeat this for the rails, but note that these will need to be cut exactly to length. Mark the mortises and tenons with a mortise gauge; when fully marked out at both ends, they should look as shown in Fig 2. The tenon marking is to the foreground, with the mortise marking out behind it. The rod is shown to the rear.

3 Use a router with a 6 mm bit to chop the mortises, remembering that the haunches are only cut to 12 mm deep (see Fig 3). Clean up the rounded ends of the mortise with a 6 mm chisel. If you have two fences for your router, one fixed to each side of the workpiece is a great help. Because the mortise in this project are cut with a router and the greatest safe depth of cut – 30 mm – is shorter than normal, the tenons will also need to be cut to this shorter length. It is, however, perfectly adequate for this size door.

FIG 3

4 Cut the cheeks and haunches with a tenon saw or a router; if you use the latter, use a guide and a block the same thickness as the workpiece to give additional support.

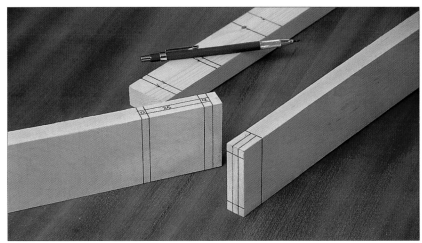

FIG 2

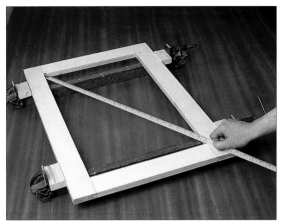

FIG 4

FIG 6

5 Dry-assemble, making sure that the frame is lying flat on the cramps, and check the frame for square (see Fig 4) – each measurement from corner to corner should be exactly the same. If not, adjust by moving one of the sash cramps slightly out of parallel, and retighten it.

7 The quickest method to mark the hinge positions is to use the old door you have already removed. Lay the doors edge to edge and transfer the marks, ensuring that the centre is the same distance from the edge as in the old door (see Fig 6).

FIG 5

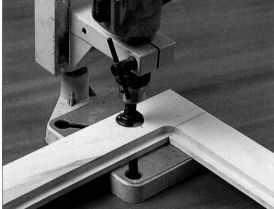

FIG 7

6 When dry, remove the frame from the cramps and lay it on the workbench. Secure and rout out the glazing rebate to a depth of 12 mm, using a rebate cutter with a guide wheel that will remove a 10 mm rebate (see Fig 5). If you are experienced at marking out, you may wish to do this step prior to following step 5. If not, doing it at this stage makes it much easier to work out what is happening. The cutter will leave radiused corners, which must be cut square with a chisel before you fit the glass.

8 Mount your drill in a drill stand and cut the holes for the hinges to the correct depth using a recessed hinge cutter (see Fig 7); in this case, the depth was 12 mm. You can use a router fitted with a 35 mm cutter to cut the hinge holes, but it is worth balancing up the cost of buying an expensive router cutter against that of a far cheaper drill cutter. Fit the glass using small maple fillets fixed in place with moulding pins. Hang the doors and adjust them by careful setting of the hinge adjusting screws.

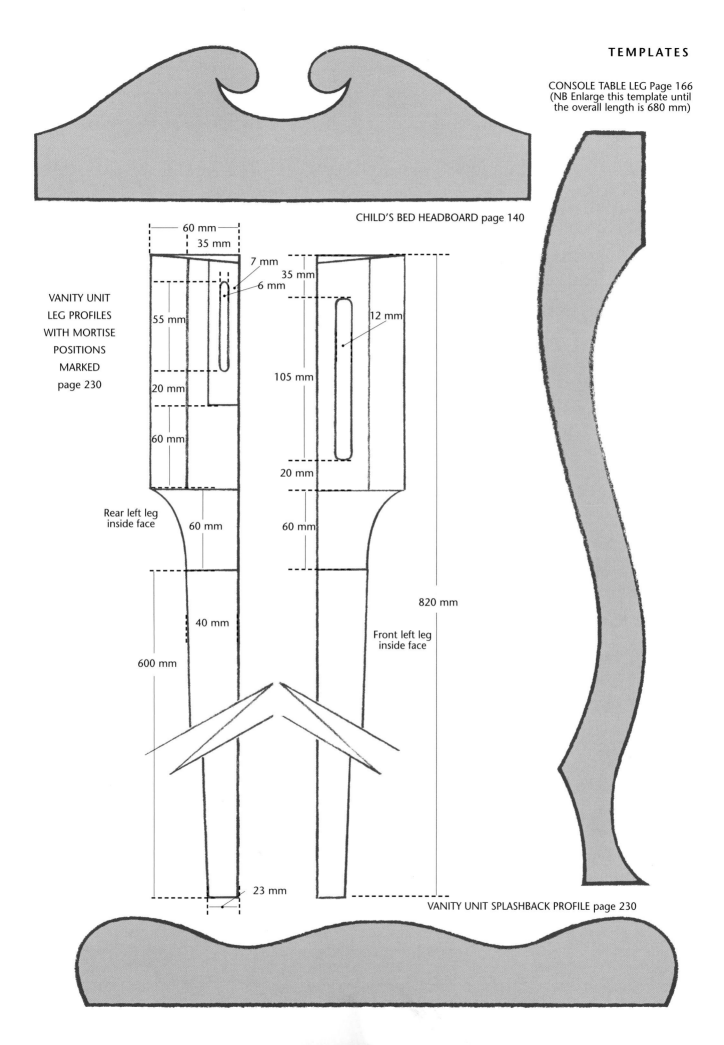

TEMPLATES

CONSOLE TABLE LEG Page 166
(NB Enlarge this template until
the overall length is 680 mm)

CHILD'S BED HEADBOARD page 140

VANITY UNIT
LEG PROFILES
WITH MORTISE
POSITIONS
MARKED
page 230

60 mm

35 mm

7 mm

6 mm

55 mm

20 mm

60 mm

35 mm

12 mm

105 mm

20 mm

60 mm

Rear left leg
inside face

60 mm

820 mm

40 mm

600 mm

Front left leg
inside face

23 mm

VANITY UNIT SPLASHBACK PROFILE page 230

SUPPLIERS

United Kingdom

General DIY Stores

B & Q plc
(outlets nationwide)
Head Office:
Portswood House
1 Hampshire Corporate Park
Chandlers Ford
Eastleigh
Hampshire
SO53 3YX
Tel: 0845 609 6688
www.diy.com

Focus DIY Ltd
(outlets nationwide)
Head Office:
Gawsworth House
Westmere Drive
Crewe
Cheshire
CW1 6XB
Tel: 01270 501 555
www.focusdiy.co.uk

Homebase Ltd
(outlets nationwide)
Head Office:
Beddington House
Railway Approach
Wallington
Surrey
SM6 0HB
Tel: 020 8784 7200
www.homebase.co.uk

Hardwood Retailers and Timberyards

North Heigham Sawmills Ltd
26 Paddock Street
Norwich
Norfolk
NR2 4TW
Tel: 01603 622 978

South London Hardwoods
390 Sydenham Road
Croydon
Surrey
CR0 2EA
Tel: 020 8683 0292

Ironmongery

Isaac Lord
185 Desborough Road
High Wycombe
Buckinghamshire
HP11 2QN
Tel: 01494 462 121

Router Tables and Accessories

Trend Machinery & Cutting
    Tools Ltd
Unit 6 St Alban's Road
Odhams Trading Estate
Watford
Hertfordshire
WD24 7TR
Tel: 01923 221 910/249 911

Tool Manufacturers

Black & Decker
210 Bath Road
Slough
Berkshire
SL1 3YD
Tel: 01753 511 234
www.blackanddecker.co.uk

Stanley UK Holdings Ltd
Sheffield Business Park
Sheffield City Airport
Europa Link
Sheffield
Yorkshire
S3 9PD
Tel: 0114 276 8888
www.stanleyworks.com

Tool Retailers

S. J. Carter Tools Ltd
74 Elmers End Road
London
SE20 7UX
Tel: 020 8659 7222

Tilgear
Bridge House
69 Station Road
Cuffley, Potters Bar
Hertfordshire
EN6 4TG
Tel: 01707 873 434

The following magazines can also provide an overview of woodworking retailers:

Furniture & Cabinet Making
The Guild of Master
    Craftsmen
166 High Street
Lewes
East Sussex
BN7 1XU
Tel: 01273 488 005
www.thegmcgroup.com

Practical Woodworking
    and *The Woodworker*
Berwick House
8–10 Knoll Rise
Orpington
Kent
BR6 0EL
Tel: 01689 899 200
www.getwoodworking.com

Traditional Woodworking
The Well House
High Street
Burton-on-Trent
Staffordshire
DE14 1JQ
Tel: 01283 742 950

South Africa

Hardware and DIY Retailers

Mica
(outlets nationwide)
Tel: 031 573 2442
www.mica.co.za

Wardkiss Paint and
    Hardware Centre
329 Sydney Road
Durban 4001
Tel: 031 205 1551

Timber Retailers

Citiwood
339 Main Reef Road
Denver 2094 (Johannesburg)
Tel: 011 622 9360

Coleman Timbers
Unit 3, Willowfield Crescent
Springfield Park Industria
    4091 (Durban)
Tel: 031 579 1565

Federated Timbers
17 McKenzie Street
Industrial Sites
Bloemfontein 9301
Tel: 051 447 3171

Penny Pinchers
261 Lansdowne Road
Claremont 7780 (Cape Town)
Tel: 021 683 0380

Timber City
74 5th Avenue
Newton Park 6045
    (Port Elizabeth)
Tel: 041 365 3586

Tool Retailers

J & J Sales
38 Argyle Street
East London 5201
Tel: 043 743 3380

Tooltrick
55A Bok Street
Pietersburg 0700
Tel: 015 295 5982

Australia

General DIY Stores

Carroll's Woodcraft Supplies
66 Murradoc Road
Drysdale
Vic 3222
Tel: 03 5251 3874
www.cws.au.com

Hardware

Boxmakers Brassware
PO Box 136 Dungog
NSW 2420
Tel 02 4992 3068
www.boxmakersbrassware.
    com.au

Mother of Pearl & Sons
    Trading
Rushcutters Bay
34–36 McLachlan Avenue
NSW 2011
Tel: 02 9332 4455

Timber Suppliers

Aw Swadling Timber &
    Hardware Pty Ltd
92–94 Lilyfield Road
Rozelle
NSW 2039
Tel: 02 9810 4177
www.hntgordon.com.au

Trend Timbers
Lot 1
Cunneen Street
Mulgrave/McGrath's Hill
NSW 2756
Tel: 02 4577 5277
www.trendtimbers.com.au

Tool Retailers

Carba-Tec Pty Ltd
(outlets nationwide)
Head Office:
40 Harries Road
Coorparoo
QLD 4151
Tel: 07 3397 2577
www.carbatec.com.au

Colen Clenton
20 Long Street
Cessnock 2325
Tel 02 4990 7956

Hare & Forbes Machinery
    House
(outlets nationwide)
Head Office:
The Junction
2 Windsor Road
Northmead
NSW 2152
Tel: 02 9890 9111
www.hareandforbes.com.au

H. N. T. Gordon & Co Classic
  Plane Makers
50 Northcott Crescent
Alstonville
NSW 2477
Tel: 612 6628 7222
www.hntgordon.com.au

Timbecon Pty Ltd
10–12 John Street
Bentley
WA 6102
Tel: 08 9356 1653
www.timbecon.com.au

The Wood Works Book &
  Tool Co
8 Railway Road
Meadowbank
NSW 2114
Tel 02 9807 7244
www.thewoodworks.com.au

New Zealand

General DIY Stores

Bunnings Warehouse
(outlets nationwide)
www.bunnings.co.nz

Hammer Hardware
(outlets nationwide)
Private Bag 102925
North Shore Mail Centre
Auckland 1330
Tel: 09 443 9953
www.hammerhardware.co.nz

Mitre 10 (New Zealand) Ltd
(outlets nationwide)
Private Bag 102925
North Shore Mail Centre
Auckland
Tel: 09 443 9900
www.mitre10.co.nz

PlaceMakers
(outlets nationwide)
Support Office:
150 Marua Road
Ellerslie
Auckland
Tel: 09 525 5100
www.placemakers.co.nz

CONVERSION CHART

To convert the metric measurements given in this book to imperial measurements, simply multiply the figure given in the text by the relevant number shown in the table alongside. Bear in mind that conversions will not necessarily work out exactly, and you will need to round the figure up or down slightly. (Do not use a combination of metric and imperial measurements – for accuracy, keep to one system.)

To convert	Multiply by
millimetres to inches	0.0394
metres to feet	3.28
metres to yards	1.093
sq millimetres to sq inches	0.00155
sq metres to sq feet	10.76
sq metres to sq yards	1.195
cu metres to cu feet	35.31
cu metres to cu yards	1.308
grams to pounds	0.0022
kilograms to pounds	2.2046
litres to gallons	0.26

INDEX